Seasons of Balance
On Creativity & Mindfulness

S. Teague & Shana Thornton

Thorncraft Publishing
Clarksville, Tennessee

Copyright © 2016 by S. Teague & Shana Thornton

All rights reserved.

First Edition, 2016

Published in the United States by Thorncraft Publishing. No part of this book may be reproduced, by any means, without written permission from the author and/or Thorncraft Publishing. Requests for permission to reproduce material from this work should be sent to Thorncraft Publishing, P.O. Box 31121, Clarksville, TN 37040.

This book is a work of art. Names, characters, incidences, and places that are the products of the authors' imaginations or used fictitiously are identified in the work, and all composite "characters" in the individual narratives retain the origin and essence of the actual event. Authors are not liable to any persons living or dead for this work of art.

ISBN-13: 978-0-9857947-9-8
ISBN-10: 0985794798

Cover Design by etcetera...
Cover photo by S. Teague, SaltH^{2}O Photography
Tree photos on title pages by S. Teague, SaltH^{2}O Photography
Author photo of Shana Thornton by Terry Morris
Author photo of S. Teague by SaltH^{2}O Photography

No part of this book cover may be reproduced, by any means, without written permission from Thorncraft Publishing.

Library of Congress Control Number: 2016931608

Thorncraft Publishing
P.O. Box 31121
Clarksville, TN 37040
http://www.thorncraftpublishing.com
thorncraftpublishing@gmail.com

10 9 8 7 6 5 4 3 2 1

DEDICATION

For you who know yourselves, congratulations.
For you who will find yourselves, be patient.
For you who don't know you are lost, you are worth finding.
—S. Teague

For women who want to risk and to create.
—Shana

CONTENTS

	Acknowledgments	i
1	Beginnings | An Introduction	3
2	Winter | Rest	5
3	Spring | Awaken	37
4	Summer | Grow	69
5	Autumn | Transform	103
6	Winter | Restore	129

ACKNOWLEDGMENTS

Thank you to those of you who helped to make this book possible by giving your time, advice, and encouragement. We are grateful for all that you do: Terry Morris for business advice; Kitty Madden for extensive reading and editing multiple versions; Beverly Fisher and Rita Yerrington for editing; Erica Trout for design; and everyone at Parnassus Books for creating a place for book lovers and for supporting our endeavors by hosting the book launch.—S. Teague & Shana

Thank you to Shana. Publisher, friend, and most important, a dream catcher. Through your dream, I awoke.—S. Teague

Thank you to Salty for saying, "Yes," to the books, and for inspiring so many people in the process. I especially thank you for being my friend.—Shana

Seasons of Balance
On Creativity & Mindfulness

1 BEGINNINGS | AN INTRODUCTION

Dear Reader,

If you could carve into this tree without harming it, what would you create? This book is a space for making your mark. You have the ability to explore your ideas and creativity through the seasons of your life. That's a gift to you. Trees change with the seasons to sustain life for themselves, and many other forms of life benefit.

As we write this text and get ready to print books, we authors have never met face-to-face. We "met" one another on Instagram, an online social photography network. The Instagram community was the impetus for some of our writings, and we are grateful for those connections and the growth they inspired. We have maintained the timeless quality of those first writings while often digging deeper in this book than Instagram's character count limitations allow. After deciding to create this book, we began to share sections on social media before the book was available. The responses from our social media readers assured us that the writings in *Seasons of Balance* were something we wanted to keep and to share beyond social media sites and their hourglasses.

We have created a book that you can read from beginning to end, or you can open it at any place and find topics and ideas to prompt further inspiration. We have divided our text into seasonal compilations to represent the nature of creativity. As one season helps us to restore our creative practices, so does another season arouse our creative endeavors and still another stimulates us to action. We need all of the seasons of our life to meet goals. Each step along the way is part of the accomplishment, leading to the next step, which is truly a revelation in every aspect of our lives. As a tree changes with the seasons so do our perspectives on many topics in life, and not simply topics about which we've formed opinions, but ways of life and ways of being in the world.

Too often, we fear the freedom to *not* compartmentalize our lives. We want to understand our lives in nice, neat little categories of defined roles, and yet we don't quite grasp how those ways of defining ourselves by role affect our meditations, relationships, fitness practices, and creative accomplishments.

We both practice yoga, and you will read about how our practices influence our creativity and vice versa. A crucial part of our creative lives and this book is our inspiration that is enhanced by physical fitness activities. We do not agree with the stereotypes that divide athletics and intellect and creativity. Categories and labels like "dumb jock" or "prima donna" do not interest us. All ballerinas and soccer players are athletes, and may be artists and scholars as well, depending upon personal interests. This mixture of artistry, intelligence, and fitness provides balance in our lives.

We invite you to explore the mixtures of your life with us in this book. We have left blank space on some pages if you want to add your drawings and/or writings. We hope you are inspired and challenged to create, to keep a daily journal of your own ideas that our book may prompt, and/or to make your world a better place by thinking differently and with more awareness.

What do you want to accomplish that is truly your life story?

We created this book with the intention of prompting ideas…answers may be ever-evolving.

Many of our topics are unrelated, but we have each created some larger sections written within each season. For example, S. Teague writes a section called Be the Change, and Shana writes a section called Gratitude. To make it easier for you to know the author of each topic, we have chosen different fonts to represent our handwriting.

We know it takes courage to boldly create from self-awareness. Be brave as you are honest with yourself.

Best wishes,
S. Teague & Shana Thornton

2 WINTER | REST

Light

Fill the dark spaces in your life with light. If you can't find light; create it, be it. —S. Teague

Preparation

As we move through days, months or even years in our practices, we experience ebbs and flows. In the beginning days of our practices, we start to bud out. Our seedlings break the soil as we find our way to the sun that is yoga. After breaking the surface, we bask in the comfort of knowing our way around the terms and the mastery of the beginning, so we see our first blooms in our practices. We water and fertilize our practices, producing beautiful summer flowerings of our skill. Crisp air of accomplishment fills the lungs of our practices. Seasoned effort is a telltale sign of autumn. Hard work and skill are obvious. Radiant splashes of color romance the feeling of achievement, just as our seasons move into our lives. Winter has moved into mine. As I felt my body preparing for its winter, I was afraid at first. I wanted my vibrant summer colors or that sharp air of my autumn practice. I was afraid that my practice would lose its flare if I allowed myself a winter. I dug deep to remember my beginning—my spring. As my practice starts to come full circle, my body craves a winter. A time to move at a slower pace. To study my practice and improve what I know. I find nourishment in my accomplishments as I allow my body time to rest. I find my breath, and I stoke the fire that is burning in my soul for my beloved. My practice. My inner fire and breath are like stacked wood in the corner. Meditation becomes my hibernation. Moving at the slower pace of restoration, I am preparing. — S. Teague

Breath and Balance

Releasing the breath is letting go...exhaling a substance (carbon dioxide) to the trees and plant life. We are letting go and giving something at the same time in almost every moment. We are receiving in the next instant, a new breath of oxygen, a measurable substance. Giving & receiving in each moment. We do it all the time, even while sleeping.

Our breath reconnects us to our bodies and place...we must be in the now when we are conscious of breathing. Too often, we think peace and balance come when we get somewhere, accomplish something, change in some way, yet all we need to do is find the balance that's already present in ourselves. Be at peace, balance with your breath, and take the time to love who you are. You are making a space for creativity to emerge. —Shana Thornton

Peace

Peace is something so precious to all of us or the word "stolen" wouldn't be used to describe the loss of it. If you put ownership to your peace, would you feel more in control of it? Would you be more willing to protect it? Like locking your vehicle when you exit, think if you kept your peace that safe. Would it change who you allowed "near" it? Protect the peace you've found in your life. Don't return to places you know it will get lost or stolen. Own your breath. Protect your peace. –S. Teague

Masks

How often we put on masks. I wore masks my whole life. I hid behind what I believed would make me acceptable. Never did the masks reveal who I truly was at the core. In 2014, just two years before writing this, I came out from behind my masks. I even wiped away my beloved mascara. I don't want anything between me and the world. I want the real deal. Now all you see is an inner reflection of my true self. Welcome.—S. Teague

Narrative | INHERITANCE

We don't decide what we inherit. If a person dies, we can sometimes pick and choose belongings they left to us. But the traits, the place, even the labels and the status that we initially inherit on the path of life are what we are born into. The debt, the fears, the hopes—often, those are passed along. Stories, told and retold from generations past, from your own youth—you file those away and keep them safe. They are part of you.

The telling of a tale infects a person who wants to learn the lessons, and from numerous people, I inherited ways of being and doing to make me, and emphasizing the women in our families feels not only important, but often overlooked by history in namesakes and so much more.

I inherited how to be an artist, first of all. One of my great-grandmothers, Hattie, lived in a little tilted shack with an outhouse until the late 1990s. She canned fruit and vegetables, chewed tobacco, and taught me how to draw roses. I vividly remember the lesson. Her last name was Thornton, and she was a master of drawing the queen flower of thorns, the rose. She began her drawing of the full rose with a squashed circle, and then encircled it with two half circles, which were surrounded by three oval-shaped petals, and so forth.

Just down the road from Hattie was Nana's brick house with flowers that were fluffed like ruffled dresses around the lawn. The fruit trees hummed and buzzed with life. I climbed the trees, made up rhymes, and watched in wonder as Nana made food. She stringed green beans and shucked corn. I could watch her fingers and arms move in unison as she peeled apples and left one long curl. I inherited a love for the beauty of home from Nana.

Next was the belief that I could surpass those women in my family who didn't graduate from high school or didn't go on to college, and they gave me that belief. My grandmother, my aunts and mother said that I would graduate from a university, that I would be the first generation of my family to earn a degree. And, with their support, I did so proudly and undeterred, and then, I went on to get another one.

An inheritance doesn't always involve death. Some inheritances come straightaway during life so that you can enjoy them together. Running was a gift given by my Mom (she's still giving it), and they traced it back...to a great-great-grandma, a Dutch woman named Jane who made the newspaper as the fastest runner in Jackson County, Tennessee that year.

Like our ancestor, my Mom loved to run. She charged up and down Pinnacle Hill Road, the pinnacle part, for miles every week while I was in elementary school. She lapped the town on New Year's Day, putting in over twenty miles, some of it in snow, with my Dad in tow. Twenty years later, I ran my first half marathon with my Mom.

I pass this on to my daughters. We run on the trails. We go in different directions and then circle back to meet in the forest. We laugh and play.

Some inheritance is reciprocal. I take my daughters to visit our wise women. When I visit her, my aunt confronts me with stories. She demands that I "step it up" because she "has a feeling." We have stayed up too late, drinking wine. She is serious, a little bleary-eyed but no less intense and not going to lose this late-night motivational moment. She knows what I should do and she will coach me to repeat, "Write the book. Write the book." She will keep me awake until I swear on every grave that I will "write the book." So, I started a publishing company and have published five books and counting. Now, I chant to other women to "write the book."

Inside my home, I see the furniture that belonged to my mother-in-law and her mother and her grandmother. I have the wooden recipe box from my husband's great-grandmother who owned a restaurant "The Sweetie Pie" in Michigan. I've never been to Michigan and they sold the diner long ago, but the photos from the 1950s show a broad woman with dark hair grinning behind the counter. Even though we never met her, we can still enjoy what she created—the smell of her brownies fills our home.

Some inheritance corrects bad habits, once and for all. During the final years of her life, my grandmother lived in a nursing home. I brought a new nail polish and painted her long fingernails, which always seemed so elegant. I grew up biting mine until they bled and the tips were swollen and tender. As my grandmother lay dying from cancer, my family surrounded her, offering our togetherness during her final days of life. She gave her bag of fingernail polish and files to me, as I held her hand. That was the last time she was capable of communicating to me during her final passage. Since that time, I have faithfully painted my fingernails and refrained from nail biting. My daughters and I paint our nails with her polish and add new colors to the bag—a bottle of blue and green—giving our own flare to a new habit.

My grandmother's quilt was sewn from scraps of dresses and tablecloths and pants—from her mother, her sisters, her children, her husband—her life covering me when I was in labor, waiting, feeling the contractions and counting them. Knowing the timing from the stories I listened to about giving birth, about that pain and beauty, the joys and losses, I waited under their wisdom until the timing was right.

I tuck my daughter's clothes into her great-grandmother's dresser drawers. We look into the same mirror. I know her great-grandmother cried here as my daughter will. She probably leaned in and applied her lipstick and eyeliner, as my daughters might do. Or, will my daughters curl their hair, shape them into Mohawks, shave their heads until smooth, or cover them with ball caps? Regardless, I hold my daughters tightly and hope that they will inherit joy and wisdom more than anything and see it reflected back to them. Because what you want to inherit is the memory of your grandma's hand holding yours, of her voice reassuring, of your Mama's loving baby-talk that never fades, of the places where you shared meals and conversations, stories and clothes. At night when you grow up and tuck yourself in and then your own family, you need the inheritance of those strong and secure, resolute women who said that you are loved and loving; you are more than you know in the beginning of your life. You are the hope and strength of all your mothers.

—Shana Thornton

What have the women in your life passed down to you? Do you consider these skills, ideas, and traits to be your inheritance?

For any of the topics we discuss in this book, no matter how long or short, we have left space for you, the reader, to add your thoughts, stories, poems, drawings, and/or plans. Sometimes, I ask questions to prompt creative ideas and mindfulness about each topic or season. Other times, it's up to you to interpret how to use a particular writing. Make this space your own, too.

Be the Change | STRONG WOMEN EMPOWER OTHER WOMEN

The magnitude of my Mother's strength defies all of my sensible logic. I have never seen her defeated, yet I know she has struggled. I have never seen her give up, though I know she's fought battles. I have never seen her without honor because she's my mother. Strong women teach other women, their daughters, friends and peers, how to navigate through life's seas with grace and admirable courage. Strong women give when there is need; they console and cry, when you need a soft heart. Strong women hold you up when you are weak even if on their last leg. Most of all, strong women build each other up, support, even when it's hard to understand. Strong women love and let love pave the way.—S. Teague

Discarding Labels

As I drop back into camel pose (ustrasana), my right knee makes contact with the floor normally causing a bit of a jolt. The head of the titanium rod that runs the length of my lower right leg clashes skin to concrete and reminds me that I still have to make slight adjustments. The amazing thing to me is that when I'm in camel correctly, the pain of my leg disappears. This is true for our hearts and minds as well. How much pain would disappear in our lives if we just made the right adjustments? If we stopped wearing the badges of the injured and broken, stopped labeling ourselves by what misfortunes we have or had? Replace them with love. Flash *your* favorite parts of you. Pin awesome to your chest. Wear the badge that shows where you are going vs. where you have been. Put on your medal of honoring you.—S. Teague

Gratitude | BEGINNING: BOREDOM

At a young writer's workshop, someone asked author Ann Patchett something like, "What's your advice to young writers who feel stuck with writer's block or they just don't know what to write about?"

Patchett's response was something like, "Go to a room where there's nothing. Make yourself as bored as possible and you'll write your way out of the boredom."

Boredom means that something beyond pattern has set in. Compromise, but beyond it...acceptance, and beyond that...doldrums and back toward the mundane with a dash of clouds, clouds, clouds, but boredom is not as potentially depressing as the endless rain. Boredom is a place of great expanse...safe space like no other in the forgetting. Boredom allows for a spark. My office is like what Ann Patchett said, very boring to me...old furniture and filing cabinets with books I wandered through too many times and in great depth. First comes the boredom, sagging in my chair before the keyboard, white paper, blank paper, legs outstretched too many days, pressed into the desk chair, falling asleep just waiting for a story, way past the point of frustration, way past the point of thinking I have it, given up, despair nonexistent, dust grabbing my attention, cracks in the drywall....Finally, with a slight start, boredom gives space to write the stories of a tree that has grown a very long time. It has enjoyed days of new bright green, reaching growth, and hurried forward, stood tall against the forces, become a force, stretched ever outward until it yawned a great long time beyond sleep perceived as boredom, and when it jostled back to awareness with the sunlight, it had grown a girth for standing strong and height for holding, and written many stories of humans, animals, insects, and plants along its trunk and branches. The boredom was so very good for opening to creation.

Many people create their tributes of gratitude during the autumn and winter months, as those months lend themselves to remembrance and slowing down. Throughout this book, I'll write about gratitude on a variety of topics and invite you, at any time throughout the year, to consider what makes you the most thankful.
—Shana Thornton

Consider now: how does boredom actually help your creativity?

Be the Change | DO IT NOW

If you aren't in love with you, right now, in this moment, what do you need to change? You're in control. Whatever popped into your head: Do it! Make that change. It's that simple, and it's your choice. ~S. Teague

Equality

How often do you "judge a book by its cover?" I was thinking back to my Anatomy and Physiology classes, and all of the different skulls and various bones we had to study. None of the tags said, "Had tattoos" or "had crazy hair and lip piercings." None said, "PhD" or "High School Drop Out." No "Black" or "Caucasian," "Male," "Female." Just "Human Skull," "Human Femur" and so on. At the very core of our makeup, we are all the same. All equal. —S. Teague

Our Seasons

Since I started living by the water, I've been afraid of the seasons changing. I haven't learned how to love the water when it's cold and uninviting. It's the same water, the same beaches that give me so much joy when the conditions suit me. So, my love for the ocean is conditional? If asked that question, I would immediately say, "No, I love the sea. Period."

I'm not being honest with myself. I wonder if I do this to people in my life as well. We all have seasons. Am I a conditional friend? When their forecast isn't to my liking, do I steer clear? We need to love them in the cold and dreary moments. In doing that, imagine how beautiful each season would become, how deep friendships would increase with each changing layer of leaves. Love to the degree that chilling winds and rain are as welcomed as sunny with zero chance of rain. —S. Teague

Breathing

BREATHE. If you seek it, you will find it. -The *simple* act of breath. So many times in my practice, I have avoided certain asanas because I couldn't find my breath. Breathing is the key that unlocks all doors. Involuntarily, our bodies insist on breath. Our first act as we are born is to breathe. Yet, in moments of fear, pain, love, excitement, good or bad, we forget our breath. Just as we involuntarily take breaths, we stop our breath in the same involuntary way. Writing this, I'm so aware of my breath. As I pause to think, I breathe in, not breathing out until my thought is complete. Do I hold onto it as comfort? As a form of controlling the moments? Obsessive concentration induced lack of oxygen. Sighs and deep breaths resume when the goal is accomplished. After forty years of daily practice, I'm still relearning to breathe. —S. Teague

A Gift

I gave myself a gift. I crave the solid ground beneath me; soles and palms connected to the earth, I found peace. I silenced the wonderings of who I am at the core. I muted the doubt that had always lurked in the dark parts of my mind. Pressing my heels down in forward fold, my fingertips danced as I found a solid handstand. Dirt, concrete, sand, and flooring are as comforting as a warm hug. I gave myself to yoga and it returned to me the woman I had been missing for years. Rooted in my practice, my soul began to open. Light started breaking into my world, affirming acceptance of my place on this Earth. We are the salt of the Earth and the light of the world. The gift... understanding. —S. Teague

Inner Firelight

During the winter, the firelight glows. The flickering grows to generate heat. It reveals the messages of your heart's desire for the year: Springtime adventures to plan, summer journeys to come. The fire grows bright as the promise of summer's blooming time.

The embers crackle and smolder, burning low, bringing reminders of the past. You contemplate how the past changed your life, put you on a route that you never expected....Maybe you never wanted the pain of disappointment. The memories give way to passion, a wandering nostalgia that burns.

The sleepy wisps of smoke fade from the final licks of flame. You listen to the last cracks and hisses from the wood. The room has grown white as ashes with stillness. You breathe in the quiet, deep with the needs of your body into the acceptance of what is, without looking forward or backward. —Shana Thornton

During the Darkness

We look into the night sky—
To see the majestic sprinkling of light.
For a reassurance that a new day will come,
That we will get another chance;
A safety net, a universal night light. —S. Teague

Gratitude | THE PAST

The past unfurls in front of and behind us, a shadow running ahead, to play, to frighten, to surprise, to delight us in the future with the choices we've made.

I've never been so aware of my gratitude for my past, as I have since nearing forty years old. Overall, my life has been a delight and adventure. Of course, like most people, I've made some choices that could have been wiser, but I find myself with little or no regrets, and that is a wonderful, albeit overwhelming, understanding. I embrace the need to improve myself, and amend the habits in my ever-changing life that don't serve me well.

My goal has been to embrace the changes of my life as they come (even if I fail in trying at times, and I do). I learned this during my first interview, with my grandmother. Her advice for having a good life was something like "learn to change as your life shows you." She said that "change," and mainly accepting it and navigating it, was the secret to success—in relationships, in business, in the self, in enjoying life. Now, I think of sailing the ocean or running a mountain trail...adapting to the changes and accepting Nature as it comes.

I'm grateful, most importantly, for people like her in my life—who made me know that I belong in the world as a person...an author, an artist, a woman, and whatever I decide to be along the way. I belong on my path and page as much as anyone belongs on theirs. We determine our own belonging. We all deserve to feel at home in the world, and part of that is accepting the past that brought us to the changing present, that will give way to the surprises of the future. —Shana Thornton

Consider how your past has both created a positive life story for you, and how you might have used your past to hinder your progress.

Do you allow your past to be an excuse to self-sabotage? How can you create a positive cycle out of your past experiences?

Manifest Awakenings

The wind does not blow me. I decide my direction. Everything I want, I will achieve. There is nothing that is out of my grasp. I manifest my destiny. I am the power behind my choices. I am anchored in solid ground. I am only affected by the tide if I choose. I enjoy the ebb and flow. My season of rest is upon me. Soon the pirate wakes.

Full on SALT. —S. Teague

Questions to Ask Yourself | TO PROGRESS

How can I change my habits and know that process will feel good?

Why do my personal changes have to be difficult for other people in my life?

How does my perception create the idea that change is difficult?

Do some activities feel good to me and benefit me that other people define as difficult?

Do I attach other people's ideas and perceptions to my life?

What is something I want to try that I or others have held me back from by making those activities seem inaccessible to me in some way...skill level, personality, time...?

Do I keep myself in defined roles and communicate only

those roles to other people who may ask me to try new creative outlets? e.g. "I'm a dancer, not a painter." — Shana Thornton

Putting in the Work & Stepping Out

Creativity can be painful at times. For writers, meeting deadlines and staying awake all night to write yet another draft is an example. We want creative outlets and forget how demanding those endeavors can become when it's time to produce our creations. Creativity isn't simply learning to pick up on the singing from the muses, as if imaginary sirens lure writers away to magically gather stories already crafted to a reader's liking. All artists must put in hours of work to become better at their crafts. If you love your art, you must learn to love the process of working to create it or you'll most likely abandon it at some future blockage or complication in your process. The trick is learning how to become better at those skills that bother you in the process of creating. For some writers, that's learning to be a better editor after they have the words on paper. Editing can enhance the words.

Consider your words to be an outfit...how you dress. The clothes you choose to wear communicate something about you to other people. The way you communicate verbally is a way to express yourself. If you take the time to go back and accessorize your communications, you can choose complementary words and phrases, just as you may choose complementary shoes or a hat. You take away and change what doesn't look good. You rearrange yourself before you step out the door. If you had the same approach to your communications, how would it change your life? What would you change about the way you speak o write, if you're a writer? If you're a painter or other type of artist, how can you enhance or fine-tune your art, make it better, add to your level of expertise? Be honest; how can you improve your craft? —Shana Thornton

Carrying the Care

I've looked past my conscience, dragged it through the mud and the muck, hauled it up a mountain, down a mountain, through a cave, gone silent with it, lain down with it in a field, fallen asleep, and awoken.

When I woke up, I knew the things that were mine and the shame that other people tried to give me, and that I worked so hard to carry and then treat, but I wasn't even supposed to be carrying those things in the first place since they were someone else's. I shouldn't have been carrying those false issues.

It's better not to take those loads in the first place, but it's part of the beginner's process—learning which are ours and which are not. The remedy is to turn those challenges over in our minds and give them true contemplation about ownership. Then, we can know which problems belong to other people and release the load, choosing to care about the revelations the conscience did reveal about the true self. —Shana Thornton

Be Like You, Not Me

My daughter told me the other day that she wanted to be just like me and that she wanted to be as good at yoga as I am. While that warmed my heart, it also left an ache in my heart. Of course I told her how sweet she was and that it meant the world to me that she wants to be like me. But I took this opportunity to nurture her individuality. I told her that I wanted her to be the best version of herself, that I wanted her to focus on whatever made her heart happy, and that being the person that she feels deep in her core is who I want her to be. I told her that I wanted to feel the same way about her, that I want to be just like her, and that I see things in her that I want to emulate. I wanted her to see that her individuality is as coveted as she sees mine to be. I want my children to see many different opportunities when they see me.

Giving my children the base knowledge in anything they choose to pursue allows me to see how they expand and grow that knowledge into a life of their own. I want them to understand they can dabble in everything or be a specialist in one thing. I want them to shy away from restriction and refuse people setting limits on them. I want them to place their mark on things. I want to help create a mindset that ends all the "what ifs" and becomes "the I dids." That's a life full of experiences with opportunities to grow their opinions. I am educating them by their own trial and error. When my children are asked what they want to be when they grow up, I want them to say, "Everything that makes me happy." —S. Teague

Lead Yourself

Be real. Be raw. Let the world see that you are human. This is what we as a human race need. We need to stop creating worlds that only exist on social media. If you can dream it, you can do it. That's why you are gifted with those dreams. They are your mental blueprints to build what you see. Dabble in everything that interests you. Stop putting a cap on your potential. Whoever promotes the idea that we can only be successful if we focus on one thing is short-sighted. Being multifaceted is the only way to go. Ride your Harley, get tattoos, go to church, give back to your community, read, paint, watch documentaries—do all that makes you feel life. Be a plumber and knit your nights away. Be whatever you want.

Don't be afraid to fail. Do so many things that you will fail. Get really scared of not ever trying the thing you are interested in because you are waiting for all the right conditions. Today is all you have, if you even make it through today. What are you waiting for? Get out of your own way. Step out of the false security of others' ideas for you. Spread your wings and do as many things as you wish, however you wish. Lead yourself into the life that was meant for you. —S. Teague

3 SPRING | AWAKEN

Pink

I like pink. It's as if red is whispering to me. —S. Teague

Claim Your "I AM"

"I am" became a very personal phrase to me during the year before writing this book. I believe that telling yourself "I am" generates your mindset. "I am" is a very powerful statement. What you think, you become. What you think, your heart feels. "I am" can be your freedom or it can be your prison. You are in charge of your "I am." You are the key to unlocking your desires, your passions, just as you are the key that locks away your fears and your doubts. How you answer your thoughts of "I am" is your choice and yours alone. You have the power to be everything you want and desire by believing in your positive affirmations of this simple phrase, "I am...."

Spend time rooting down into your now and find a new "I am." Repeat this encouraging "I am" to yourself every time you are met with a negative, be it from yourself or the world around you. Be gentle and kind to yourself by cancelling out that darkness with your own light—you have that power. Take a deep breath, and find your peace. Breathe that balance that comes with confidence. Now, shine.

Root down, find your balance, and breathe. Let the words come to you. I Am.... —S. Teague

Gratitude | HARDSHIPS

Hardships first bring pain and, later, new perspectives. In the beginnings, hardships cause stumbles before we accept solutions. Reacting to minor difficulties with anger propels situations into something worse than is necessary. Hardships do not have to equal tragedies, depending on how we handle the challenges. Firefly pose (tittibhasana, also known in English as Insect pose) reminds us to put a signal out there, flashing your light to others who may help and who will share their light to help make yours stronger. Fireflies find one another with mutual light signals. Even a light that is dimmed or harmed can send a signal to others. Through the darkness of hardships, allow your light to flash anyway, dealing with the pain, understanding it if possible, and accepting that temporary time of challenge. Later, after you heal, you are able to offer help to others in times of hardship, to see the signals of dimming lights and guide them to safety and love. —Shana Thornton

Progress | Stronger Than Before

Injured
Broken leg
Titanium rod
Yoga
Last resort
Jackpot
Body healing
Life altered.
Broken pieces
Turned into
Whole
Stronger than before
Again
Fractured
Pause
Moments of stillness
Back to my mat
Meditated healing
Restoring
Healed
Stronger than before
Mind and body
Collaboration
Unstoppable
My Yoga Body
and Mind. —S. Teague

Narrative | FREEDOM TO CREATE

Often, we are creating the best stories as we go along without a plan, and those are the most sustaining. Along the way, they can become the journeys that we doubt the most, and sometimes, we abandon those dreams and our freedom to create by doubting whether our final product or plan will be successful.

Creative freedom is actually scary for most people. You have to put yourself out on a stage, into a medium, and share an expression in words or pictures or both: A voice. A poem. A conversation. A storyline. I became a women's literature publisher to create a platform for stories to be told by people whose stories need to be in the world and who weren't receiving the opportunity. I was one of those people at the time, and the beginning was exciting, but the next steps contained terrifying moments in the life of an artist.

I learned the steps, often with awkward movements, but I learned to create books, and then I had an idea about yoga. How many ideas have you had and tossed aside later? I was finished with that mentality, and started to gather the threads that my brain wanted to weave into my life. Suddenly, I found myself really wanting to make the yoga t-shirts after coming up with the idea in a brainstorming session with a friend.

The doubts in my head materialized as people in my life questioned why I was spending my time on yoga shirts. However, my love of yoga was longstanding and growing, even though I had never expected it to factor into my business. So often, ideas are there, but we don't see the path to make a real tangible product out of some ideas. When the opportunity presented itself to create a physical object that I could wear, I didn't hesitate in finding companies I respected and going for it. My daughters and I experienced mystical moments when we came up with the trademark name of BreatheYourOmBalance, so I went forward. I reassured myself that I was doing the right thing, regardless of peoples' desired limitations on me.

 The day the shirts finally arrived, I didn't feel that fighting spirit. Like any creative, I doubted the idea of my imagination and creativity once it was tangible. I asked myself useless, doubtful questions and those negative doubts overtook my pride in all the hard work I had gone through to create a product.

 Despite my doubts, I put on one of the shirts and drove to a polling location to participate in early voting for an election. Before leaving, I meditated, asking for a sign that my idea had a place in the world. I needed to feel a connectedness, but I wasn't sure what I was looking for, though I drove to the polling location with my eyes peeled for any type of "difference"--anything out of the ordinary defined as a "sign" by me. My polling location was a local community church, and nothing extraordinary happened on my way there. Doubts invaded all my thoughts, and I crossed my arms self-consciously over my t-shirt. Of course, my t-shirt could have been one purchased at any yoga studio, but I was so focused on my insecurities that I wasn't thinking in a broader context. Inside the polling location, I waited. A woman held a baby on her hip in line in front of me. She turned and mouthed something to the elder of two children sitting against the wall, and I hadn't noticed them until that moment. The younger was seated in Lotus (padmasana), palms facing the ceiling, eyes closed, chanting, "Om, Om, Om, Om, Om, Om."

I pinched myself. I did! A hard pinch on my forearm. I could feel it, and that was my sign.

Even though I had the yoga t-shirts, I knew there was more to create with BreatheYourOmBalance, but I wasn't sure what it would be. My mind wandered. After months of posting online and joining yoga challenges on Instagram, I got up my courage to ask a few yogis to host a yoga challenge called #BreatheYourOmBalance. The yoga challenge was another step, but I still didn't know where it was leading me.

For the challenge, I asked a friend to participate in my photographs, and we went with our families to Centennial Park in Nashville for a yoga photo session and play day. I wanted to choose a powerful place that added meaning to my life. For part of my childhood, my family lived a few miles away from Centennial Park in Nashville. The park is the site of the Tennessee Centennial Exposition of 1897. After the Exposition, they decided to preserve the Parthenon and create a city park. My family moved outside the city when I was nine, but I have been visiting the Parthenon and the park for my entire life. For the photos with my friend, I wanted to invoke the power of change and shape-shifting, transformation into something more than expected. I also wanted to honor Athena, the Greek Goddess of wisdom, whose magnificent statue is housed in the Parthenon.

We stood in front of the Parthenon for Mountain pose (tadasana) with our daughters. Many participants in yoga challenges complain about "easy" or beginner asanas in challenges. I chose to include Mountain because all too often people underestimate the Mountain, or they take their own abilities for granted and forget that some people or they themselves struggle to stand. It's like when you set off on a hike, thinking only of the beauty and the epiphanies, and forgetting the trials, blisters, summits and depths of the trail. The trail has pain to offer as well, a trying of your patience, and molding you into a more comfortable version of yourself. The same is true of Mountain pose. We underestimate it, take for granted that it will be easy and there for us when we finish sun salutation. I've bobbled in Mountain pose more often than I can express. I've had to slow down and focus just to stand straight up on both feet and be there: No more moving and flying and stretching back and forth. Centered and grounded. Standing.

It's not easy to stay there sometimes, to climb back up to Mountain in a flow. Just as hiking a mountain isn't easy and doesn't always offer sure footing. Balancing on the mountain with both feet planted isn't possible in every location on the mountain. Those jagged peaks, those rolling rocks, the icy snow...in yoga, those are my shaky legs after balance postures, those are my wobbly arms after practicing crow pose (bakasana), my slippery sweat in my eyes stinging and burning, and my stretched back that wants to sway and swoon after backbends. Mountain forces me back up, reconnecting with my slower breath, with my centering to find both feet planted.

Another meaningful "beginner" yoga posture is Tree pose (vrksasana). It feels natural and ancient to my body, and yet reminds me that balance is never the same. Our ability to balance changes as our circumstances change. I am reminded of my grandfather—after surviving brain cancer, one side of his body was completely immobile and the other side was capable of incredible balance. His breath held the key to moving and propelled him forward. I watched him intently from the time I was five years old, as he struggled to learn everything anew and with all his strength placed on one side of his body. He was a part-time carpenter before cancer, and I loved the smell of the trees being made into some new piece of furniture for someone's home. My publishing company is named after this resilient inspiration. When I considered all of the meanings of BreatheYourOmBalance in my life, I knew that his example influenced another aspect of my creativity.

The trees provide our balance in the ecosystem, in nature all around us. Many people feel automatically at ease in the presence of trees, and seek their shelter in the city, so that we can breathe and enjoy natural space. To balance in tree pose is an anchoring. One leg holds you like a deep root, breathing through to the ground and out your limbs like an open mouth, taking in easy breaths.

Part of getting close to balance is learning from others who are better at some ways of balancing and who can teach and inspire us to be better people. I struggle with Lizard pose (utthan pristhasana), with sinking down and lengthening all the way through to my fingertips. I want to curl up in some way and stop the flow of this asana. My friend has breathed into Lizard pose until she is comfortable with the length and stretch. Her approach is careful and full of very deep breaths, while I shorten and pant in my breath at times, wiggling and struggling with my shoulders and forearm placement. I'm easily frustrated with myself in this asana. I lower down into child's pose to accept where I am now, over and over again, and all the while my friend breathes with deep patience and kind eyes, waiting for me to match her balance in our practice together.

I was humbled by how much I learned in the first BreatheYourOmBalance yoga challenge. When I read the responses on Instagram, I was in awe of how much the participants shared and that they wrote from the heart. The creativity of yoga in my life was on the cusp of growing again. The trademark was officially registered, so I asked, What is Thorncraft Publishing going to create with BreatheYourOmBalance beyond t-shirts and yoga challenges? My expectations were far surpassed already. And then, the obvious answer hit me during one of my runs—create a book—a compilation of writings about yoga by a variety of people. Take submissions.

As each day had progressed in the challenge, I read more and more writings by Instagram yogis & students about breath, balance, and their yoga practices. I enjoyed reading them.

I questioned whether or not a creative writing-based yoga book would be welcomed by the yoga community and the rest of the world. I looked through my friends' accounts on Instagram. Would anyone be interested in trying to make this happen with me? Could I find a contributing author? Finally, after going back and forth with the idea, late one night, I sent the message to S. Teague that I had written in my head at least a dozen times. I waited...for about ten minutes, when I received a big, all caps, YES! from Salty. Forward momentum was much faster than I anticipated. We sparked all kinds of plans and ideas. While Salty and I made the announcements to take submissions, and she began creating new yoga challenges, another idea branched off in my mind. The creativity was churning between us. This book, Seasons of Balance, came into view. I could see its meaning and structure. Salty and I talked every week, and I connected with her about creative ideas like no one in my life ever before.

Again, big questions with doubts showed their fangs in my mind. I dug in with doubts about nonfiction, if Salty would want to co-author, if she thought our writing matched, if, if, if...the ifs were digging a grave for the project. I had to jump off the cliff soon or allow the project to be buried alive, so I jumped. S. Teague screamed, "Hell Yes!" caught my hand in midflight, and was happy to jump right alongside me.

I might have destroyed many projects by allowing fear to cast doubt on the very first one and failing to allow it to become a reality. Several times since that first decision, I've made another choice to create an idea into something tangible and stamp out my fears. Despite a host of reasons for "why not" in the beginning of an idea, the reasons why you should become apparent during the journey. The true reasons why you should create are usually not illumined at the start, and you will never know the reasons why if you don't create the first steps of the journey. —Shana Thornton

Do you have a narrative about freedom in your life, and how have you or others tried to limit your *accomplishments?*

Gratitude | PARENTS

My parents believe in transformation and have always made me believe that I could make a difference in the world simply by being a kind person and striving to reach my goals. My parents have fostered love and support by sharing that they have always thought I was capable of more than I believed in myself, and that they will give their best advice without insisting that I be like them. And that's critical, the knowledge that I don't have to be like someone else, especially them, my own parents, and yet, they still support me wholeheartedly; and in so many ways, my goals are to be more like them as parents. My parents are potters, and they transform clay into beautiful and useful objects. My parents have helped me to see the power in not only transformation but in encouraging other people to find and use their talents. — Shana Thornton

Gratitude | TECHNOLOGY

We live in the world that Ray Bradbury imagined...we can communicate with our homes and the appliances within it, and the computers talk to one another to communicate messages for people. Many of us wouldn't have the jobs we have if it weren't for the advances of technology.

Bradbury imagined that those advancements came with a price, and he created all kinds of dystopian scenarios that technology and humans might make (make is an interesting verb since most of those creations resulted in complete destruction of humankind and/or human freedom) in his stories. Yet, that humans and technology might create that dystopian future is what he tried to show. That legacy of dystopian stories has been passed down in more books and films. And yet, that doesn't have to happen, nor has it. We can create a better world with technology, and people are doing just that—trying to implement renewable energy strategies in societies to alleviate the burden on people and the earth—to curb pollution and get serious about preservation because technology has truly allowed us to observe almost the whole world and the changes taking place on a global level.

On a simpler level, I am thankful that I can press a couple of buttons and brew coffee at a specific time. I can design a book on a laptop and send it through cyberspace to a printer and distributor. We can create an image without film processing. Countless programmable devices are whirring inside our homes, and that technology makes the creative life so much more convenient. —Shana Thornton

Be the Change | ENVIRONMENT

The biggest impact I believe I can have on our environment is helping those who apparently cannot help themselves. Humans continue to confound me on a daily basis. How can you look out into a magnificent body of water and toss your trash into it? Did you know that sea turtles will mistake floating plastic bottles and trash as food? Not a good diet choice. So, I do a small part to protect something dear to my heart by picking up trash on the beach near me. Stop thinking of our environment on a scale that seems untouchable. Every bit of your effort matters. Every bottle, every can. —S. Teague

Gratitude | P L A Y

Joy. Light. Children laugh. Awe. Breathe. Balance. Topple over. Giggle. Shhhhh, but giggle again and again. Try for stillness. Talking giggles. Clouds blowing. Wind whirling hair. High heels kicked off. Bare feet laughter. Bending in a laugh. Open heart. Letting go of this body's self consciousness. Rise on tiptoes. People smiling, laughing, joking...."Beautiful" someone watches and says of your play. You smile knowing you already got the moment inside and it didn't matter anymore what anyone thought. Not even you. Transcendent play.

While I think yoga often leads many people to mindfulness in a different way, yoga has helped me to be free with play. Contemplation and meditation feel natural to me—they suit my personality without strife. The yoga poses (or asana) have created a more playful space in my daily life. Playfulness in motion, by using my body, is not as fitting naturally to my everyday way, or it wasn't, until I let go to share that experience...just to have fun. Play creates an opening for others to join, especially my children. —Shana Thornton

Creating the Soul of a Bird

I wear my tattoos like jewelry. They all have a story like war medals to a soldier. With each drop of ink, every line, my feelings are mapped out on my body. With some, I made a conscious decision to put it in a place so obvious I won't forget. They're no different than the positive or affirming quotes you tape to your mirrors or highlight in your favorite books. "I never saw a wild thing sorry for itself." A sparrow flying above the quotation is permanent on my right wrist. A quote by DH Lawrence reminds me that feeling sorry for oneself is a human emotion. A grand error. Every creature in the world has a will to survive and thrive. We are taught to feel sorry for ourselves. We are taught that we have a right to make excuses. I don't want to live that way. I want to thrive! If I get knocked down, I want to rise up. Over and over and over. I will not stop nor will I quit because someone says it's ok or it's not. If you are an enabler of weakness, shame on you. Be the type of person that pushes greatness. Promote feelings of rising above the ashes like a great phoenix. Encourage yourself to be unstoppable and surround yourself with the like-minded. "I never saw a wild thing sorry for itself. A small bird will drop frozen dead from a bough without ever having felt sorry for itself." I want to create with the soul of a bird. —S. Teague

25 Cents at a Time

How often do you think you know someone only for them to throw you for a loop? No matter how close-knit you keep your circle, you never truly know what people think of you. Even the people that you trust are capable of being unfaithful friends. Is this the standard? Is it my bad judge of character? I am very intuitive. I often feel things happening long before they do. My perception is never wrong, but why do I ignore those signs? I ignore them because I want to believe in people. I want to believe that when people seem kind and loving to you it is because they mean it. Why else would someone waste their time? The truth always comes out. Always. Why waste my time and theirs if they really didn't want to be my friend in the first place? I mean, hell, I am ok with that. Nine times out of ten, I do not seek friendships out. Nine times out of ten, I get burned. The pattern is remarkable to me. I am forty years old and again, I find myself wondering if my friends are my friends. I can count on one hand who my real friends are. At times, that makes me sad and at other times, I am thankful for that. I would rather have a handful of quarters than a handful of pennies. I do not collect friends, and I don't want to be collected. I want true friendships that are trusting and last. 25 cents at a time. -S. Teague

Be the Change | BANDAGES

Bandages on my heart
Medicated with happiness,
Covering the hurt of times past.
Wounds too big.
Ineffective treatment plan.
Survival mode.
Tearing the bandages,
Searching for healing
Exposure.
Air mixes with light
Still beating.
More light,
More breathing.
Steady beating.
Healing. –S. Teague

Joy | Reaction

Everyday happiness is a choice. Every day you have multiple chances to make the choice to be happy. It's about how you choose to view the world. You are thinking... *it is not that simple.* Yes, it is. It is your choice how you deal with everything in your life. You are in that much control. It is that simple. Being scared and being angry are still acceptable. It's acceptable to get mad, to let something hurt you. It's how you react that matters. Your reaction is what defines your happiness. It's what you put out into the world. Your choice on how to deal and react will make or break your joy. Regardless of the pain you might have to smile at, it will change your life. Every positive reaction will build up your immunity to negatives. Choose happiness, choose to react with joy, and spread love with every choice. -S. Teague

Forget Writer's "Block" | (wink, wink...at 3 a.m.)

"They are good writers," you think of your favorite authors and stories. You have something to say as well. Don't try to write like them. Don't tell their stories again. Listen to your voice and story. Let the stories swell in your head and yearn to get out. Allow the story to sink into your ribs and knock, knock, knock around until it comes through your collar and arms and fingertips...the story soaks you through in the night, when you wake sometimes suddenly, sometimes wide-eyed in awe, confusion, or enlightenment. You must move with the story, carrying it quickly, sometimes cradling it so you don't lose that Rembrandt light, so perfect and fading in the real-world kitchen and smells from the night before, and ignoring those dishes of distraction, thoughts of coffee tempting you, whining of the dog who has sensed your stirring and has his own demands. Ignore it all. Get there...to the page and capture any scraps that remain and begin to write those parts of the story. Strike a match briefly. Form smoke. Alert the dawn of your fingers. When it's there, the day will come as it does anyway, with chores and habits, so stick with your story as long as possible. The clock times everything. —Shana Thornton

The Rain's Commitment

"I haven't felt the rain fall on me in a long time," he said.
   We walked under a steady rain.
   Gray horizon. Wet fields.
   Clouds swept up the raindrops in a swift dance
   through the tree branches, plopping into the river,
   soaking our clothes,
   but we don't run away from anything.
We get drenched. —Shana Thornton

Questions to Ask Yourself | TO CREATE

When do you feel most beautiful?

Where do you feel at home?

Who are the people who communicate the sense that you belong in the world?

What activities give you a feeling of bliss?

Who or what are your muses?
Do you need those muses to change over time?

Do you devalue the muses from your past in order to justify why you need a different muse?

If your muse is a person,
   If your muse is a group of people,
   If your muse is an animal,
   If your muse is a place,
   If your muse is an activity,
   If your muse is a thing,
   If your muse is an idea,
  how do you show your gratitude beyond your creative expression?

Do you honor your creative ideas by writing them down, singing them, painting them, baking them...creating them in whatever way that allows them to be something you can share?

—Shana Thornton

Artist's Magic

There are times when I take photos
I can see the soul of my subject
So brightly...
It's all I can focus on.
Being a mechanical-type artist, to see past the structure,
Get a glimpse of the life in my subject,
Is a true gift to me.
When my art opens up and allows me in,
The depth of the connection is immeasurable.
This is where the stories begin for me.
Translating subjects into souls and lines into art.
This is my craft, my magic. —S. Teague

Trail Running Messages

While running, I let go. Thoughts arrive, and I'm more accepting of them. During the run, I'm less critical of my natural creative flow. In fact, I recorded this on my phone while running so that I would say it with fluidity. It's like a bird flying, gliding, knowing where it wants to go, just being free in mind, while my heart beats, while my arms and legs move and the trail shakes out in front of me, down around me. The run is uncontainable. It sweats out the energy of the imagination and creates footprints and motion on a path, imprints of ideas in my mind, and that translates into belief in my potential, in my ancient ability and need to move as a human body, to have emotion, to be strong in that free flow. You don't have to run to be that way. You just need a vehicle that frees you. —Shana Thornton

Magic

I will always believe in magic. It's found in the sunlight glinting off a dragonfly's wings as it whirls among the wild roses and Queen Anne's lace...

It's the Queen Anne's lace holding cups of late spring, sudden snow...

It's the ironweed reflecting snowflakes of frost, fields shining blue, purple, gray, crystal frost breath. Fields sparkling up into the trees, dripping ice...

It's in the silence of ice-covered flower buds that eventually melt, and we only glimpse this silence for a moment until the sudden, vibrant hum...

It's in rhythmic work of bees combing the clover with intonations of satisfaction flying back and forth to the hive...

It's in the rainbow of leaves made by trees during the fall, a quilt of colors stitched together across the horizon, covering the gulch and vista...

It's down in the gulch where all the smooth stones are worn over time, soft, slippery, subdued, nestled, knocking together when the waters rage, making music...

It's the waters that make everything music—the rocks of the falls, the trickling passageways, the dripping from the leaves, the press of ocean on sand. —Shana Thornton

Music

I find it interesting that many people need to listen to music during their runs or workouts. They actually depend on the music to raise their energy level or maintain it. This shows how much we use creative vehicles to motivate us to create something ourselves. We depend on another energy to shift our own to such an extent that we complete tasks that otherwise seem or feel difficult (like running a marathon for some people).

The music we choose inspires us with its energy. People are the same. Do the people in your life project an energy that is motivational...that keeps you going during the difficult times, that you can count on to sing you through together...?

The people who are like your favorite kinds of music, enrich your life with powerful, bold creations, and impress upon you the energy to find harmony.

For most of the time that I've been running, I haven't listened to music during my runs. I motivate myself from the pace of my own energy. For me, listening to music changes the energy of my run, and sometimes it can be invigorating, but other times, it distracts me from my natural rhythm.

My writer's brain uses the running time to write. I run for the whole process—the freedom to create, the imagination to roam wildly, the commitment of a story playing over and over in my head. If I don't run, I don't create the initial space to write. Of course, good writing

does not come through every time. In fact, I spend the majority of my thoughts during the run looking around, observing and listening to nature, and tapping into the music I hear being made by all of the life in the forest.
—Shana Thornton

Stories to Pass the Time

When I tell a story to anyone, or even if it's in my own head, it's practice. If you can keep yourself hooked on those stories and some of your ever-changing storylines, then you should write those down and find out if they resonate with other people, too.

I lose track of time when I tell a story. It's a perfect way to evaporate time when you're bored or anxious to get on to the next moment. Telling a story is one of the best things you can do to occupy yourself or other people. The power of the story has the ability to transform. Often, it's as simple as finding yourself, by the end of the story, at the time that you were waiting for before the story started.

Many of the best stories ever written are about losing track of the passage of time by an enchanted story, being carried over to the next stage by the story or the storyteller. You can think of many stories like this— <u>The Canterbury Tales</u>, <u>The Arabian Nights: Tales of 1,001 Nights</u>, and especially children's tales and movies... <u>Alice in Wonderland</u>, <u>The NeverEnding Story</u>, <u>The Adventures of Sharkboy and Lavagirl</u> are a few examples.

With my children, I tell stories to distract them and soothe them as much as to entertain them. Allow yourself to get lost in your imagination, and begin by telling a story to children or some other willing and eager listeners. My children also enjoy making up stories to tell me.

Whenever you get stuck, just go with the first thing that

pops into your head and create from there. That's the only way to become a storyteller. Wander around until you find your characters, setting, or plot...even your genre, if you have one. Find someplace where you need to pass the time and you'll tell better stories. —Shana Thornton

4 SUMMER | GROW

Self Worth

Allowing others to determine your worth is the same as letting them use your toothbrush. —S. Teague

The Writer's Dream

I dreamt of writing like Hemingway and of being a Tolstoy. I marveled at the craft of conjuring words into paths that lead people to create alternate worlds in their minds. I dreamt of my words having power. That reading my words could fix ailments like a good batch of soup. That reading my words would cause the reader to grasp the book and pull it to their chest as if to hug the feeling I just sparked in them. I dreamt of seeing my name on the spine of a book and in a card catalog. I've read, "New York Times Best Selling Author" and said that will be me. Yet, I just remembered that I dreamt these dreams. I'm not even sure when. But they are so real to me that I feel as if it was last night. I am on the path that I had dreamt of only. On a path that was never mapped out. A path that leads me home. —S. Teague

Enough with the Good Enough

Good enough. As in, "I am NOT good enough..." This has been a nemesis. A fear inside, allowing it to motivate. The "not good enough" fear can incorporate itself into any aspect of life. The "not good enough" challenge is not better or bettering... It is feeling compelled to push more, keep going, and become more than and more than and more than....It's all about the vicious self that drives self-destructive behavior. This voice is difficult to reach for him or her or them. This voice that is part of you, because you listen to it, is smart about protecting its license to threaten you. —Shana Thornton

Art Freedom

Refuse many labels given to you by others. Believe in your creative ideas and don't allow others to squash them by limitation or "concern"—that word is often used to derail you from believing in your ideas. Why should anyone be "concerned" with my art and creativity? Why should I stop my artwork to make it more _____ for someone else? Add any term that someone has used to stop you from creating.

Despite any negativity, it is a breakthrough to persevere, create, refuse to be defined, and allow art to flow freely in and out of my life without always needing a reason, an end in sight, a commission, or a life-changing work. —Shana Thornton

Mirror Image

Take a good hard look at yourself. Do you see what the mirror reflects or is that image manipulated by the thoughts in your head? Are you kind to yourself or are you your own biggest critic? Are you accepting of the fact that you are a fantastic work in progress, ever-changing and uniquely you? Or are you harsh with your thoughts because you set worldly standards for yourself that most likely are impossible to meet? I challenge you to accept the beauty that is you. Put down those images of distorted perfection and bask in the inner light that only you radiate. -S. Teague

Beauty Judgments

I have rebelled against stereotypical beauty as long as I can remember. It is one of the few things that remained the same my entire life. Long blonde hair, dyed it black. Long lovely locks, shaved them off. Makeup or no makeup. Take me as I am or don't. The only place that I stayed true to myself was in my appearance. Pushing limits is me to my deepest core. Appearance is only a facet of that. I always found it so sad that people spent hours on their appearance to be acceptable to people that were living under the same rules of scrutiny as themselves. Whom do they impress? What is the purpose? Who is making these rules? Purple hair isn't acceptable because it isn't a natural hair color. Well, neither is blonde with massive dark roots. Noses cannot be pierced but earlobes can. Tattoos are frowned upon but cherry-red lipstick is considered sexy. People accept what seems natural when a typical woman's beauty regimen is anything but natural. Her beautifully curled locks came from a curling iron. Her straight smooth hair came from a flat iron. That acceptable girl altered her natural self. She spent an hour and a half getting ready to be acceptable to the world. Her "natural" beauty takes work and a lot of it. I would be willing to bet that 80 percent of women look different in the mornings than they did the night before. I don't. But I am the freak. I am the unnatural one. I go to bed and wake up virtually the same. I choose not to wear makeup. I chose to have dreads in my hair or a Mohawk but with each of those I am me. Do you think a woman feels like herself when she can't remember her natural hair color or she won't go into public without putting her "face" on? I have been told, "You don't have to push every limit." Oh, hell yes, I do. I do because the status quo is so wrong and so altered that appearance is what people judge you by. Never judge a book by its cover.

    I want real people in my life. Real friends and real enemies. I grew up in a town where everyone was nice to everyone. Smiling to your face and talking behind your back. That is the worst form of abuse. I have found that if I am true to myself, I push limits with my appearance. It's probably one true trait of who I truly am. In my later years I have found it as a useful method to who I want to have in my life. I find people that judge by appearance will probably never be a true friend in my book. Those that are embarrassed to be seen with me out of fear of judgment of themselves aren't worth my effort to create a lasting friendship. I give everyone an opportunity. I even do this unknowingly. By being off the status quo rocker I am either approached by open-minded people or I am ignored by the closed-minded ones. This is a new lesson learned by me. I cannot think of a time that I looked at anyone and formed an opinion. People's looks are the last thing on my mind. I watch people's actions and I listen to the words they speak. My judgment of others is action-based. I find that most people who aren't "normal" to the eye are very normal at heart. They are usually very open and loving. They aren't judgmental and don't pass judgment. They are more apt to be "live-and-let-live" in nature. Truth of the matter is this. People that pass judgment on appearance will more than likely pass judgment on other parts of your life. Are some people willing and okay with having judgment passed on them? Maybe. But, I am not. I want to let people wear their hair as they wish and the clothes that make them feel their best. The last thing I would ever want is for someone to try their best and then I shoot them down without a second thought to why they chose what they did. We all have a reason for why we do things. We have all been hurt and are recovering from something. I am a fucking judgment rebel. Hear me roar.
—S. Teague

Gratitude | IMAGINATION

Imagination is the spark in the dark & the light. Imagination is risk...making it up, creating a new space, characters, and worlds. Reaching back, up, down & into the abyss at once, I find the cadence & rhythm that is my imagination! I am thankful to create...to imagine for fun that which disappears and to imagine for real that which becomes. To make something tangible out of imagination brings it out of the abyss of mind and into the light of the world.

How much do other people tell you to think and feel, instead of waiting for your responses, and how much do you respond based on how you think you should instead of allowing for creative expressions, even and especially during times of imagination and insight? —Shana Thornton

Be the Change | FOOD SECURITY

This is a tough subject for me. I view food as fuel. It's not a comfort for me or an indulgence. I tend to eat very raw. I am 80% fruit-based but am very cool with having a steak if my body wants it. My biggest issue is waste that I see when it comes to food. Texas has a restaurant that is an all-you-can-eat massive buffet. I don't believe in the old philosophy of "You must eat everything on your plate." The amount of food that is left on plates and thrown in the trash saddens me. I wonder if it could be used as fertilizer, just something besides trash. Gluttony runs rampant in the US. Super size this. Mega size that. Eat all you can and just toss the rest. How can we stop the "eyes bigger than stomach" mentality with our children? By teaching that you should only take what you need and if possible, give back to the world. Healthy eating habits translate to a healthier, and more equally fed, society. Next time go for one helping, not two. Buy and cook only what you will eat. Save the leftovers. Mega size your love for others by downsizing your plate. Every bite counts to someone who gets none.
—S. Teague

Gratitude | F O O D

Until the middle of the last century, many people in my family worked as farmers. One of their major crops was sugarcane. Sugarcane is the world's largest agriculture crop by production, according to the United Nations' Food & Agriculture Organization (as of a January 2015 report). It was once a major crop in the US Southeast, until the last century, when many U.S. farmers had to find other jobs.

I am thankful that as a child, I could still witness the experiences of farmers and the difficult life they lived to bring local food to local tables. Food brings people together with other people and with nature when they get to know the sources of their food. Each bite is a former plant or animal...made up of their parts—each bite and drink is energy—life grown and accumulated with nutrients and moisture, time and effort, patience and toil, texture and life force. I am thankful for the sacrifices made to provide food to me and my family.

At dinner time in my family, we go around the table and tell something joyful and something challenging about our day. We also speak a blessing or hope for someone or something else, be it a family member, stranger, friend, community, tree, field, animals, etc. Food brings us together and we discuss life around the table. We eat. We commune together at this time—talking, sharing, and eating. Food is the work of sun and soil, farmers and plants, parents and cooks. —Shana Thornton

Be the Change | ACCESS TO SAFE WATER

I'm going to be honest. I have no idea what it's like to not have safe water. It's such a foreign concept to me that it's even hard to imagine. I was impacted internally because of the awareness awakened by the seven-day Instagram challenge to make a change in the world hosted by @109world and @yoga_girl. Because of these awakenings, my life will reflect externally all that I have learned. Imagine if these ideas weren't just focused on for seven days. If everyone focused as we did for the "challenge" on Instagram and other social media sites, the difference, the changes, we could make would be life-changing, life-giving, and sustainable. I'm supposed to be discussing "safe water," but my heart and mind are overwhelmed with commitment to actually be part of something that could change people's lives. We are to be the change we want to see in the world. —S. Teague

The Mirror

The earth
Our human bodies
Are mirroring it
The metaphors are parallels
Of mountains and valleys
Of pleasure and pain
Of change and transformation,
of places that seem to remain the same
Of disease and waste
Of pollution and overuse
Of treasured space and hallowed ground
Of possession and freedom
Of responsibility and commitment

The earth
Being of life and death
Reflections in the waters
Muscles and tendons
Birth

Heartbeats and blood circulating in a heated rhythm
Cancerous invaders and growing tumors
Garbage dumps to fill the land
Oceans and pastures
Corporate ownership to buy what one wants
Obligation to pay the bills
To bring in the tide

Swallow whole cultures and schools of fish
Erupt in a wild dance
Bursting forth a radiant lava
Cooling into stone and ash
—Shana Thornton

The Good Times

We want the good times to last! And last! And last! ...Until we move on to different good times. Yeah! And last and last...More good times!

I've been in that phase—trying to stay in an exhaustive wave of what makes my life "a good time." Thankfully, I am evolving that phase, so good times happen every day in small ways. Good times exist in complex dilemmas. To find the good times in life's challenges offers a way to sustain me. Yet, it's one of the hardest things to do. Frustration culminates until I want to shout, "Now!? Again?! This absurd madness of humans?!" Ahhhhh! We all feel this anguish over the realization that nothing can pacify the effects of what is churning on from the catastrophic errors of those before us. Additionally, we fictionalize futures of complete annihilation or brutality or revert backward/forward in a caveperson-ish, alien-ish existence. Extinction isn't so farfetched. The rest of these fear-based theories/stories lack. They lack a lot to be believable.

I am thankful for people who look for ways to correct past mistakes that weren't theirs to begin with but they don't care about that--they find the good times in the present and keep going. Mourning is necessary for some people. Getting up close and personal with the cynicism and the bad news of our time is the game of others. As difficult as it can be to accept, those good times are in all of that...in the middle. —Shana Thornton

Giving, but Not Wanting to Receive

I've lived a life of choosing to be the giver instead of the receiver. I love how it feels to gift someone something. I love to make others feel good. I love to see them excited and know that I created that feeling in them. I love supporting and cheering on someone. From my words to gifts, I wanted to be on the giving end. I view the reactions from people as my gift. It's a high for me. A selfish one.

As much as I love to give, I hated receiving. The feelings weren't the same if I was on the receiving end. It made me self-conscious and nervous. Receiving in a graceful manner is hard for me. I am so transparent. I cannot fake excitement or joy over something.

So, I was always in a state of panic until I realized that I was taking the joy of giving away from someone else. Light bulb! By not being open to receiving what someone had for me, I was denying them the thing that I loved so much. I realized that other people wanted to make me feel good as well. Allowing them to give to me was allowing them to feel the joy that I thrive on. I'm still learning to be a graceful receiver, and I am learning to see that my reaction is their gift. Smile, and the thanks come very easily in that way of thinking. –S. Teague

Gratitude | FRIENDSHIP

I cherish the unwavering loyalty and dedication of my truest friends, and how we support and love one another through the changes of life. We listen. We offer advice. We laugh. We listen to music. We sing. We tell stories. We make music. We jump for joy. We high five. We hold hands. We ask questions and receive answers from one another. We walk together. We celebrate. We cry. We hold onto each other and we let go to travel our own paths and return with stories & gifts. We love. These are the friendships of the soul, returning again and again, no matter where life takes you. These friendships follow through the years, shadows of the past, and continued influences of togetherness.

I value the friendships that didn't last, too. I learned lessons about my own boundaries and what I'm willing to do for a friend, and what some friends are incapable of giving over years and seasons. There are profound lessons in friendships that last only one season with someone because they leave your life. Some people are merely passing through—a shooting star of influence. Some friends are taken by death too early, and leave a scar of grief and mourning for what might have been. Other friendships show a mysterious and elusive light that you don't understand for years to come.

Friendship offers a metamorphosis....Sometimes a competitor becomes a friend or a friend is secretly conspiring against you in some way. These are friendships that startle with insight, teaching us how to listen to our intuition about people, showing us our own incorrect judgments, and even more, how to establish safe boundaries when a friendship is uncertain to us.

Friendship is ultimately a risk to love and give your time and energy to another person because you like their company. —Shana Thornton

Gratitude | FREEDOM

Freedom is a security and a gift that I wish for everyone. Growing up, I definitely took my freedom for granted. Now, when I run or walk the trails at a park or close to my house, freely, every day, wearing whatever I want, speaking as I want, openly, about any subject, I am reminded that I am free and grateful to all who have sacrificed to make that possible. On my trail runs, I actually say "thank you" aloud to the U.S. servicemen and women who sacrificed and continue to daily. They cannot hear me, but I say it in my heart. Many members of my family have served in the armed forces and continue to now, and I live in a community just miles from a military post, where I am reminded of the sacrifices. Daily, I see women and men in uniform and their families.

While I am an American and have been privileged to live in a wealthy country, I am aware of the lack of freedom in other parts of the world. I'm aware of how fragile our societies actually are. The novel <u>Running the Rift</u> by Naomi Benaron reminds me that so many people make freedom possible. It's about the 1994 genocide in Rwanda and the cultural climate and events leading up to it. The control and oppression would be devastating, and I cannot imagine the fear of living with curfews and divisive propaganda.

The week after reading Benaron's book, I traveled with my daughters and my Mom, and we saw a bald eagle fly over us. I felt the symbolism of freedom over us, enabling women to travel alone without fear. There are many societies in which women cannot travel alone and/or they cannot dress as they want, and so many more limitations. In the Acknowledgements to her novel, Benaron declares that no people on earth should have to endure genocide or the methods of separation leading to such acts. Like her, I also wish for a transformation so that the devastating parts of human history do not repeat.

I feel gratitude to people all over the world who make sacrifices for freedom, including those who write stories and songs about freedom. The art that expresses freedom is critical in communicating that basic human desire—to be free. —Shana Thornton

Listening | Summer Sounds

The escape of nature gives us another song—
running the trails I hear the crunch of fallen leaves,
stories of summer from high in the branches of trees
have floated down,
the chirping of birds, their calls and songs,
the laughs and drumming of woodpeckers,
the shrieks and hoots from raptors
gliding above the river
and along the rocks of the bluffs,
the crickets' invitations in the meadow grasses,
the whispering of the wind along the passages
the deer beds carved into the tall ironweed,
and the river bluffs carry the echoes of wild ducks.
I love the run,
as each step is transformative,
enchanting with nature's songs.
This way of listening, I free myself to have space
in my head to write and listen. —Shana Thornton

Superhero

I've always had a fascination with superheroes. I love their super-human strength and special powers. The majority come from some sort of trauma or drama-filled childhood. They have transformed being an oddball into an amaze-ball. They never fear not being able to take care of themselves or those they love.

People crave for them to be around and look at them for their strengths, not weaknesses. Take Superman; no one ever says, "Oh great, it's just Superman. Hope that no one has any kryptonite, that big wimp." They cheer for his greatness, not his weaknesses. Yet, we are all aware that each superhero has weaknesses. I've spent a lot of my life looking for a hero because I was convinced that I wasn't one. I don't have super-human strength...or do I? I don't have special powers...right?

I can hold my own bodyweight on my fingertips, if I wish. I can love unconditionally and receive love unconditionally. Aren't those things similar? Sometimes it's not a cape but a mala. Sometimes it's not bending steel with your eyes but warming someone's heart with kindness. Sometimes you have to step back and take a good hard positive look at yourself to realize you have a touch of destiny about you. We all do. So today, I double-dog dare you to make yourself epic because sometimes we have to be our own superheroes. —S. Teague

Yoga in Public Spaces

Lights twinkle from the solarium ceiling. People stare up into the lights...the glittering, and moving shoulder to shoulder up the escalators. Do you ever notice how our actions create a change of energy in a place? I've noticed how an angry person can shift a group's dynamics, and how one act of kindness can bring a group together. Yoga in public spaces, even one asana through a series of breaths, creates a pause, a serene energy. —Shana Thornton

The Now

There in the past & there in the future are ships set free. Ripples of water sent out. "Here" is in the midst. "The Now" always runs on and on, constantly moving away to a new "Now." Stillness is a passing fantasy. "The Now" always has form, sound, time, and not time. It is the elusive present, the phantom so many people chase. The idea of the "Now" is simple. Living the "Now" is complex. It's the ultimate individual riddle.

Accept. Why is that so challenging? Be here. Why do we constantly have to retrain ourselves to be here? In the past, I argued with myself about my mindfulness, telling myself to be even more mindful until that demand left me with debilitating contemplation. Too much "Am I in the present moment?" and then not knowing how to proceed. Of course, I am living my present every moment. Now, if the present leads me to a focus on a future goal or a memory, I don't fight it anymore, and I live it without apology to myself or anyone else. I cannot stress enough my present focus for writing this book—to feel at home in the world as I am, as we are. Now. —Shana Thornton

Narrative | CLASSROOM MEDITATION

One of my first teaching jobs was a summer program with advanced placement high school students who were taking college preparatory classes at the university where I was a graduate student. I was teaching literature, and my objective was to introduce the students to literary terms and interpretations of texts via literary criticism.

For the first class on the first day, I followed a standard textbook and typical professorial procedures. They were instantly bored but played along as advanced students have learned to do...that's one unspoken reason why they're advanced. I had been one of these students, I realized as the class ended, and I groaned at the thought of continuing for six weeks with tests of literary terms and papers that could be as boring as my lectures.

I started with the second class, but something happened inside. I had an idea about the poetry I was going to assign for the night's reading. I had a crazy idea to do a guided meditation, introduce the students to their totem animals, and ask them about the symbolism for animals. These ideas came quickly, little flashes of daring, risky insights. I finished my introduction, complete with the rubric and list of assignments. Then, I asked the students to get comfortable at their desks, close their eyes, and follow along on the meditation I was going to guide them through, if they wanted. A few of them looked skeptical, as if I might do something terrible to them while their eyes were closed.

"This does connect to your assignment and to literature. I'm not going to hurt you, I promise." A few students laughed and said that we hadn't built this kind of trust in our relationship yet, but they would do it anyway.

I went through a guided meditation, slowly, and deliberately. First, I asked the students to close their eyes and listen to their breath. I asked them to breathe deeply a few times, and then to listen to the sounds in the room. I named some of the obvious sounds in the room. I told them to breathe again...a few deep breaths. Visualize the color blue, I said, and named some obvious blues in nature—the sky, the ocean, iris flowers. Now, visualize the blue becoming purple, I said, and named violets, purple onions, a deep sunset. Visualize green, I said, like the leaves and the grass. The green takes you somewhere and now, you are outside in nature. You are safe. Look at everything around you. Get a good look. Remember that you are safe. Now, you will see an animal coming toward you or looking at you. It can be any animal, and it is there to meet you. What is the animal like and what does it do? Does it offer anything to you? Do you offer anything to the animal? Take some deep breaths.

After a few more prompts, I mentioned the colors again, but in reverse. I asked the students to become aware of their surroundings, to listen for the sounds of the room again and their own breathing.

They were captivated. Every student closed their eyes. Each student seemed sincerely interested in the meditation. They were eager to share their experiences. "What did it mean?" they asked.

I asked them, "What do you know about horses?" when one student told us she had "seen" a horse. The students looked confused. "What does a horse represent to you?" I asked a student.

"Speed," he said.

"Yes," I said. "What else?"

"Power. That's why they always say, 'horsepower' to describe engines."

The class progressed from there, and we shared the meanings of animal totems by describing them to one another. I gave them poetry that mentioned or referenced animals, including passages from the I Ching and Tao te Ching translations.

That summer, all of my classes moved with tranquility as we spent the first part of class in guided, and sometimes silent, meditations. The students were more cooperative and responsive than in any classes I've taught to date.

Yet, I spent a great deal of my time during the summer in a state of worry. My anxiety about teaching in this way almost caused me to change my strategy. It was the enthusiasm of the students that kept me going. I thought that my bosses would call me into their offices to say that I should return to more traditional teaching methods. That call never came. In fact, at the end of the summer, the students had a small banquet. Each of the teachers gave out awards for Most Improved student, Most Creative, etc. To our surprise, the students had decided to make their own awards for the teachers as well. This was not part of the plan. I was most shocked and humbled to receive the award from the students for the Most Intelligent teacher. I assured my colleagues that this was not the case, as I knew all of them to be adept in their fields of study. One of the students said, "It wasn't that you know so much more than any of the other teachers, Miss Thornton. It's that you kept saying that you learn as much from us as we do from you. You taught us how to think, and you let us teach each other."

Whenever I have doubts about following my intuition and breaking from a traditional way of doing something, I recall that summer when it felt like I took a big leap into the mysteries of learning with my students.
—Shana Thornton

Questions to Ask Yourself | S Y M B O L S

What symbols have value in your life?

How do you use those symbols to motivate you? And, do you see those symbols directly reflected in your artwork and/or your way of life?

Have you carried certain symbols throughout your life?
Where did you first pick them up?
Did someone introduce you to them?

Have you tried to pass on your value of certain symbols to your children or to students or friends and relatives?

How are other people's interpretations of a symbol you value, part of your story?

Do you view these symbols differently than the way other people or societies view these symbols? How does that affect how you use the symbol in your art or way of life?
—Shana Thornton

Gratitude | FITNESS

I don't think fitness works for everyone as a creative motivator. I don't think everyone feels inspired when they workout physically. For some artistic people, they don't want the physical invigoration in that way.

I am a person who needs to be physically active in more than one way in order to create with the most awareness in other ways. Trail running and yoga are the practices I choose most often in order to be in my best state of mindfulness. This is not only true about how physical fitness affects my creative endeavors, but also my social interactions. I have less social anxiety and am more open to people and different social settings if I've completed a run and/or a yoga practice.

In my past, I was unaware of how much I need the physical practices to be mentally, socially, and spiritually healthy. —Shana Thornton

Physical Fitness Fit & Balance

I'm writing to the average person when it comes to fitness. I'm not trying to be a physical fitness expert...I don't want a certification or to put 100-mile races and triathlons and ironmans under my belt. I don't have that kind of experience. I do have the experience of keeping my fitness and mindfulness practice every day, even if it's only for ten minutes of a yoga flow on days that are busy with work and playing with the children, helping with homework, making meals, and more. There are plenty of days when my running and yoga practices are longer—an hour or two because those days allowed for that. I've also learned how to play with my kids and do yoga or get in part of my run, and to space it out when I can grab it.

I'm not a person who enjoys competition with fitness, whether that's running or yoga. I prefer charity events if I do public runs or yoga challenges, or events without prizes. The competition part of both practices gives me anxiety and takes away the flow that I find. Races and highly competitive challenges and events are not good for me, and I've had to realize this by trial and error. I went through many processes to try to work through my issues and find the motivation that I saw other people emanate. Still, competition wasn't for me. I can now have a physical fitness practice that brings me balance and keeps me motivated and interested.

The key is finding what works in your life to bring balance and move you in a positive direction. For some people, running races and winning prizes for yoga challenges could be motivators that drive their passion to continue. It's personal and not always based on the social trend or standard. —Shana Thornton

The Earth is Alive

The earth teaches me everything about blessings and agonies, desires and losses.

The warm sun's heat. The spark of the fire. The ice of the waters. The rough prickles of the grass. The melodic scratching of the branches. The cool moisture of the dirt.

The earth speaks and teaches me the story of everything. The earth has a multitude of scars, accepting human dreams and demons, holding onto them for us. By the earth's ancient example, we accept all the mysteries that we might never know.

We must love anyway. —Shana Thornton

How the Soul Savors

Sometimes on the trail, I don't do any planning or think about anything contemplative or life-changing; I run. Somewhere in the clouds, in the trees and sky, I see momentum everywhere. Somewhere in my body is motion. Sometimes beautiful lines come—little story scenes, poems and ideas—and they flutter away, and there's no capturing any of them. I have no desire to capture. There's only the letting go. I savor some memories for my own soul. I don't always want a document or a camera. — Shana Thornton

Efficiency

Efficiency can be the death of craftsmanship. Corner diners are sold into franchises. Custom built homes are replaced with cookie cutter houses. Mass production meets a projected demand. In the effort to have everything, we are losing our individuality. We are losing the craftsmanship that helps us remain a society of individuals versus a society of sheeple (people + sheep = sheeple). Mass efficiency has caused a mass identity crisis. Custom and one-of-a-kind have become relics. Whether we like it or not, mass production becomes the only option many people have. I don't want to live in a world where the only difference in my life and someone else's are the numbers on my house. That visual may appear drastic, but imagine if creativity and originality don't become more important than the bottom line. —S. Teague

5 AUTUMN | TRANSFORM

Adaptation

Being your own hero requires you to adapt and create anew when out of your comfort zone. —Shana Thornton

Gratitude | H O M E

Home is my refuge and sanctuary. I yearned for our own place for the first years of our marriage when my husband and I were students and then, during our first jobs after college. I wanted a home close to the wildlife of Tennessee, where my children could have space.

During the summer and fall, a homeless man stood at an intersection that we passed through on our way to my older daughter's school. He held a cardboard sign that weathered as the year passed. We gave him money and food when we could maneuver across traffic to him. It's a busy intersection, and trying to reach him was dangerous. When the weather became colder, he wasn't there and we wondered about him, if he would seek a shelter to spend the night or if he lived in a tent we had seen nearby.

Around the same time, we passed through a neighborhood with 5,000+-square-ft homes, and my daughter said, "I wish we had one of these huge mansions, don't you?"

No, I shook my head. The houses were massive structures with small yards in the middle of the city. I wanted her to understand that people make a choice about what they put into the world. I said, "We made a choice. I never wanted a house so big that we would be strangers. It's not practical. It wastes energy to live like that." I went on to give examples of how a huge house wastes energy.

She gave me a disgusted look at first and then gazed

out the window, thinking about what I said. We continued to her school, which is located beside federal housing projects. That night at dinner, she talked about her friends who don't like where they live, and some who are ashamed of their homes. She said, "That homeless man would love to have my friend's house...or mine."

This is simply something we all must learn—to be grateful for what we have even if it isn't our ideal, and to realize that my ideal home isn't someone else's. Yet, at the end of the day, we all simply want a refuge and sanctuary to call our own. —Shana Thornton

Process of Now

Now, this journey.
Building blocks, love notes of now,
Your foundation.
Every morsel of progress, slow and steady or natural talent.
All essential.
Breathe in each step,
Find your stories,
Build memories.
Learn to love you in these moments
And your relationship with your practice.
Allow
A love affair of mind and body.
Passion in the process.
Be a warrior and lover of your now. —S. Teague

Gratitude | QUIET

Morning frost on the fields sparkles in sunlight. Everything vibrates blissfully through the quiet space. The peaceful hum of nature and the quiet of the hallways in our homes are solace before everything bustles into the day. This time of year gives space for watching. Sometimes, our inner warrior must seek and make a space for quiet. I often need to turn off the chatter of the television and radio, the media, the phones and notifications, and simply be. I like it when my inner voice that incessantly wants to create and solve is finally quiet, too. —Shana Thornton

I'm Still Here

Silence was torture.
Quiet seemed a death sentence.
Being alone in my mind with just my thoughts terrified me.
Racing down the highway, music blared.
TV, Radio a constant companion to aid
In the drowning of my mind.
I was afraid to be alone with myself.
Afraid of what I would have to face.
Reality. Me.
I was afraid I would have to answer to myself all the whys.
Allowing so much to engulf me, I self-medicated with noise.
"Bang your head, mental health'll drive ya mad." Not this girl.
It was all that was keeping me sane.
I ran and ran from the quiet until one day the noise overtook me.
Blaring in my head, I couldn't find myself.
I couldn't gather my thoughts.
Clawing for silence, begging the noise to stop.
A void.
A loud vanishing whisper...silence happened.
I heard my heartbeat.
I heard my breath.
I closed my eyes,
I heard my voice...I'm still here.
Quiet.   —S. Teague

Gratitude | DIVERSITY

Diversity gives us life. Without diversity, the planet wouldn't exist. Too many species rely on one another and aren't similar or even related. We, humans, need differences, as much as the planet needs variety. There are infinite combinations of fingerprints, snowflakes, chains of DNA. Even if we look alike, we don't think the same, and our bodies are not identical even if an identical twin.

I'm baffled that people, at times whole societies in history and even now, believe that one "type" of people and way of life is the only way. Life is diversity. Diversity of thinking and being is what makes life. Diversity prevails, and hallelujah for that. —Shana Thornton

Same Cloth. Broken Mold

Cut from the same cloth. Broken mold. I've filled both of these positions in my family, an imposter in my own skin. I felt if I followed the same cloth pattern that life would somehow be easier. Learn by example. Yet, I always pushed. Always. Trying to break out of the bolt of family cloth. I sought to break the mold. Done. Mold broken. Stripped of the garments of my lineage, yet empty. Uprooted, I was lonely. I missed my fabric. Why! How? I'm a rebel. I'm one of a kind. Damn right, I am. Also very wrong. To be myself, I felt I had to bleach my material. Color my own. I did. Resulting in the exact pattern I was born with. My cloth cut from the same. I just wanted to wear it my way. -S. Teague

Gratitude | MENTORS

Mentors have the potential to point the way through the darkness with words and actions and to coax our best creative expressions into the light. My mentors have inspired me to believe in my potential, to see life from another perspective, and reflect life as I experience it. I wasn't always conscious of choosing my mentors, and most were professors or colleagues. They've pushed me beyond my comfort zone, and challenged me to make the world a better place by using my talents and education as well as treating others with kindness. Some of my mentors have been vital to a particular time in my life or a project, while others are a constant anchor in the midst of life's movements. Some mentors and I have parted ways for good, changing and moving in different directions. Regardless, I'm open to the lessons that brought me awareness from all of my mentors.

Making mentors into perfect people happens often, but it's untrue and unnecessary, as mentors are imperfect. Mistaking a mentor for a perfectionist is the sign of an immature presumption about roles in relationships. The mentor is flawed and will show you their weaknesses over the course of the relationship, and that's part of the acceptance of our humanity, our shared roles. As you have strengthened your own talents because of the wisdom gained from the mentor, you honor both yourself and your mentor by becoming a mentor to someone else.

Mentor relationships are special and sacred, rare even, and should make us pause to pay homage to the wise offerings we have received from others, even if and especially when their wisdom is briefly passing through our lives, for it has the potential to offer resonance never before known to us. —Shana Thornton

Autumn Arms

The strength I feel when I am in an arm balance during my yoga practice has no comparison. The sense of accomplishment fills me. The arms and hands that I have done countless acts with are my tools. They have fulfilled me by loving my babies, cleaning my house, and holding the hand of the one I love. Holding the weight of my world. These arms and hands have lifted me out of hurt. These arms and hands have embraced people who are no longer with me. Arms and hands have folded across my chest in sadness and shown my excitement in victory. They have folded in prayer as I sought out answers. They are the source of my gravity defiance. They are my warmth and where my richest colors lie. They show my scars and my strengths. They bear my creativity and are the canvas of my life story and my yoga journey. My practice begins and ends with my arm balances, my alpha and my omega. Arm balances are where my seasoned postures lie, the fall colors of my practice. They are my depth and my vibrancy, jewel tones. They hold the comfort of warm days but the excitement of the crisp wind. Arm balance is the color splash of my hard work. My autumn. —S. Teague

Gratitude | I N D I V I D U A L I T Y

Raining for days....Autumn rain.
Fuzzy seeds cling to stalks of plants
For this long after summer,
After the harvest,
Enduring a steady pouring from the sky.
The group of cream-colored seeds forms
A cluster of bright potential
Against the brown, wet landscape.
How difficult it can be
To maintain our light in a downpour.
A tree golden with leaves still shines
When many of the others have dropped their crowns.
Progress from spring through summer into autumn.
Disappearing into soil, nutrients again for the tree,
The plants drink and make seeds. —Shana Thornton

Be the Change | INVESTING in CHILDREN

I have always looked at my three children with the realization that in raising them, I am raising adults. That the teaching they receive today will be the way they navigate the world. All the while, I am wanting them to be well educated, self sufficient, and confident. I want them to be compassionate, giving, and humble. I want them to know they are the light of the world, to know that is a gift and, at the same time, a great responsibility. I want them to run and play as all pirates should, but also have an inner peace of knowing they are loved and respected for who they were made to be.

I am only your guide, my crew, the journey is yours. —S. Teague

Gratitude | EDUCATION

My education has been bolstered by the idea that everyone deserves to learn what they want, and it doesn't have to take place in traditional schools by traditional means. But my story is just that—I was lucky to have an extended formal education, in which I could explore my ideas, and I wish it for everyone who wants it—to choose and go as far as you make the effort with learning and in the setting that you choose. I felt at home in the university setting, where the learning environment was positive, encouraging, and engaging.

I discovered my voice first at the campus newspaper. I used it and discovered quickly how to share that opportunity with others. I was hooked on writing with groups of people and creating publications. During graduate school, I found my mentors in the creative writing program and women's studies classes, and in the developmental studies department where I began to teach college courses with a woman who was lively, and inspired everyone to reach their greatest potential. These were educators who were taking new classes themselves. They were traveling, learning, and sharing.

I found an inspiring message often on campus, and perhaps that's one reason I didn't feel my dreams were out of reach. My education wasn't easy, and my life work wouldn't be either. Many people and places have the potential to educate us about the human experience and the earth itself. And then by our own knowledge gained, *we have the opportunity to give back.* —Shana Thornton

Be the Change | EDUCATION FOR ALL

I've been lucky to have amazing teachers in my life, from elementary, junior high, and high school teachers, to college professors that numbed my brain out with endless opportunities to learn. I have a couple I wish that I could thank again, but they are no longer with us. The most influential teachers are my three dirty-footed monsters. A few years ago, I became their teacher, after deciding that homeschooling was the best option for our family. In teaching them, I've learned more about them and myself. I'm thankful for the gift of knowing they are being educated to the best of my ability, and that they won't fall through the cracks. I am responsible for creating the want to learn in them. They seek knowledge and input. They crave discovering new things. Through them, the world takes on many new shapes.

Thank you, crew. You've taught me more than you'll ever know. — S. Teague

Gratitude | M O J O

He smiles even when times aren't golden.
When we point and tell him, "Get out,"
and he thinks we aren't nice at all
as he slinks around the corner
with lowered head, he doesn't lose the smile.
He revels in motion to practice his craft,
his deep signal to let me know
that he watches the shadows.
He remembers being almost starved before we met,
fur matted after a beating,
and the rescue. No grudges now,
but he doesn't recall it for me. I gave him a home
after the passage. He looks out the window,
a sentinel at his post, sniffing the air.
His golden hair shines
in the light. —Shana Thornton

Tribute to Veterans

Ships are safe in harbor, but that's not what ships are for. By the end of today, 22 veterans will have committed suicide. That was the statistic on Instagram in 2015 for a challenge called #22aday, and the purpose was to bring awareness to the growing suicide rate among U.S. military veterans.

Many times we look for fictional characters to be our heroes. I'm very guilty of this. It's no secret; I love comicstrip superheroes. I can respect both sides, and some villains need love, too. Who doesn't love The Joker?

I was reflecting on my superhero obsession. They have all derived from some sort of adversity. Most were mortals that have overcome major pain and mental scarring. We hold them up and call them heroes. We cheer in their triumphs and root them on when the going gets tough. We get goosebumps, perhaps a bit starstruck, at their bravery and selfless acts to protect the world around them. Why? Because we can relate to pain and hurt. Because we all feel we deserve to rise out of the depths and conquer our darkness.

What if we looked at our military as we do comicstrip characters? What if wearing a USMC/Army/Navy or Air Force hoodie got the reaction that a Batman or Superman hoodie does? What if we treated our nation's heroes like the true heroes? I wonder if we would still lose twenty-two of them to suicide every damn day. Don't they deserve our loyalty as much as Clark Kent or Bruce Wayne?

I personally don't care if you are for or against war. I don't care if you are Republican, Democrat, or Libertarian. Makes no difference to me if you watch Fox News or CNN. What matters to me are the people who made a choice to defend your right to have an opinion. Those are the people who give you the freedom to be pro or con on anything. Those heroes chose to put their lives on the line so you could go to sleep at night feeling safe. I've lost friends to war. I have friends who have lost loved ones and friends. I've seen lives that seem to be cut short because of war. I also know that everyone we lost made the decision to fight for their country. They felt that sense of duty to defend the freedom they know. That's honorable. We have heroes coming home every day that continue to fight that battle. Men and women who put their lives on the line for us. We lose twenty-two of those to a bigger enemy every day, suicide. Reach out and tell a veteran thank you, today. It could make all the difference.

After a few days into the challenge on Instagram, I realized that we lost 132 veterans to suicide. By the end of the next day, that number would rise to 154 suicides. That's 154 real people who swore to protect and defend you and me, and now, the number has grown into the thousands since 2015. Yes, it's personal. Spread love to all you come in contact with today. You could be touching a hero that needs just a glimpse of your light. Kindness and love can make a difference. —S. Teague

Narrative | A WRITER'S PROCESS

After years of being a student and completing assignments, some with excitement and even zeal, and others with a mindless meeting of the requirements, I was unaware of my writing patterns unless they pertained to an essay for an assignment. Literary criticism was my focus, and so my writing was dependent upon other books and essays. I read, evaluated, made connections, and wrote the essay using the texts and other critics as evidence.

I didn't know anything about my creative writing process, yet I filled journals with creative writing and artwork. I dreamt of writing from my imagination, but I wouldn't allow it to grow into a possibility for my future craft, and dare I think, employment. Then, it happened. I had somehow managed to square away my life and secure my home life with my first daughter, and carve out writing time for my escape. I ran with it.

Truly, I started running as a hobby and a character study, as my character for my first novel became a runner in the book, and I needed to write from some experience. It's funny to me that people see the main character from that novel, Ellen, as so much a part of me, and I only see that we share some of the same interests, just as I would with any other character or person who has a daughter and a running hobby. I disagree with many of the ways the character of Ellen sees the world, and I would hope that I would handle the cards Ellen was dealt much differently than she did, but I also wrote her character with a great deal of compassion and gave her a voice because I thought it was worthy of being heard.

After that first novel, <u>Multiple Exposure</u>, and the mistakes and triumphs it brought for me, I was ready to understand my writing habits and get serious about what worked in my life. I wanted to strengthen my writing life.

One of my first insights was that I needed to read and talk about literature as I did during school, but without writing formal essays about the literature. Once I was full of reading and contemplating stories, I turned to written correspondence, and I noticed this had been a major writing outlet since third grade, when I was given a pen pal at school. I maintained quite regular correspondence with her from eight years old until the start of college, and can remember sometimes practicing my fiction skills (embellishing and making shit up) in the letters I wrote to her.

Letter writing is still essential to my process, even if I only write a handful and the correspondence fades, as it does now in our internet era. And sadly, many of my letter-writing relatives have died, and it's a dying art to sit down with pen and paper and address that to someone. Luckily, I do have two friends dedicated to writing letters when that cycle moves into my life. We strike up wherever we left off...I don't ever feel bad when I fail to respond, because we switch up often enough with spaces of silence. Of course, those delays always make the letters more interesting and lively, with chances for more stories to tell. Letter writing is my way of getting my personal life and stories out of my system and away from pages in books. My imagination is then free to roam without the burden of needing to relate nonfiction. I can get to the magic of fiction and create new characters and stories.

Writing this book has been the nonfiction part of my process, and it's new for me to share it outside of short writings on blogs. I haven't written my usual letters to my two friends—I've written here, to you.

The next part of my writing process has evolved and now includes my running habit. I did keep that habit, and my reverence for nature during my runs creates a space for the muses of inspiration to reach me with stories. My mind is free to roam, and my imagination goes wild. I let it flicker like a fire while I run and don't judge the thoughts or their patterns.

Stories worth telling don't always emerge. Some thoughts have words and some don't. Some visions are explainable, and some linger in mystery. Others are discarded. Many mental searches for stories are like sitting in front of a blank page. The story comes when you aren't really searching...maybe you're in the process, but so much has happened that you've forgotten, and you've suspended your belief and disbelief about a story at all, and then, it reveals itself with a glimmer. Those are the stories I chase so that I can retrieve the gem that started in the middle of a long run up a big hill, and it was the one that I want to tell, that I have a passion to chase down and put on the page. I want it to be alive. That's when I know that a piece of fiction is ready to start taking control of my writing time.
—Shana Thornton

Remembrance

Sun showers us with remembrance.
Seeds fly from the dried wildflower stems.
A cold wind rattles through the fields and lets us know
with a shiver what is coming.
The winds push the birds across the sky —
the geese take flight under the clouds,
trusting one another to get there
together. —Shana Thornton

Questions to Ask Yourself | R E F L E C T I O N S

Do you consider the autumn of your life, and do you try to bring the same vitality to all the stages of your life?

Or, have you valued a certain age of your life above others, either in longing to get to that age or in longing to return to a particular age?

Do certain arts recharge your creativity? Music? Art? Performances?

If you seek a lot of entertainment and a wide variety, do types of art affect you differently?

Do you alter your interests and activities because of your age? Do you define some activities and interests as youthful and others as mature? Does this affect how you have fun?

Are you capable of being creative and being playful at the same time? Or, does creating your artwork require you to be serious? What if you mixed it up—created something serious if you're usually playful, and vice versa...? Have you tried getting out of your comfort zone more than once? Rarely do we create art that we like on the first attempt, so try a new creative approach a few times to get the feel for it and allow for the possibility of a new creative endeavor to emerge. —Shana Thornton

Feel Something

Do you restrict yourself emotionally? Do you feel emotions and allow them to run their course, or do you limit the time you allow yourself to feel emotions? Do you meter your reactions? Do others' emotions make you uncomfortable so much that you don't allow them to have the needed time to recover or rejoice? When did it become the standard to emotionally cap ourselves? In doing this, we have caused ourselves and others to harbor and push through emotions that make us personally uncomfortable.

Even in our celebrations, we are taught that we cannot be overindulgent in our excitement and happiness for ourselves or we are seen as self-absorbed. We live in a world where excessive celebration in sports will get you penalized. Why are we allowing ourselves to be told we can't cry and we can't celebrate? We should feel the moment, feel our way through the situation.

Cry! As long as you want, be a weeping sack on the floor.

Get excited! Slam that football down, run around before the crowd, shoot off your imaginary pistols in the air, and pump those arms in celebration.

Feel something! Stop numbing out emotions with restrictions from a robotic society. Feel everything to your heart's content. I wonder how quickly we could stop packing up our emotional baggage if we just left all of it in the moments surrounding the events of our lives? —S. Teague

6 WINTER | RESTORE

Passage of Time

Times of darkness will pass just as seasons do. Choose to step into the light and move forward. Stay one step ahead and light will prevail. Never forget the darkness, as it is a reminder of how bright your light shines. —S. Teague

Respect Rest

PUSH your body.
Skim the LIMITS of your abilities to do killer postures day in and day out.
RIDE that adrenaline rush of nailing a goal asana.
FEEL that high.
LISTEN to your machine.
HEAR the need for rest that your BODY makes clear.
RESPECT the call to RESTORE.
REST. —S. Teague

Mental Winter

Winter came to my practice fast this year. Almost as if overnight, I went dormant. I searched to understand my lack of desire to push myself. I took a day off, and that day turned into three. I had to make myself get on my mat. What was this? I hadn't experienced this feeling from my practice before. Hell, I hadn't experienced this in myself before.

In the past, if I hit a winter in anything else in my life, I would immediately go find brilliant fun summer colors somewhere else. But, not with my yoga practice. I wanted to figure out why I was so disinterested. Leaving my practice would be leaving a huge part of me. I would be unfinished. Nothing could replace that missing piece. I decided to go into meditation. There, I resolved to search out the softer side of yoga. I decided to yoga my mind. I practiced restorative postures. Sitting in the calm of the mind, I now had complete control. The other seasons of my practice taught my mind to control my body. Winter in my practice has taught my body to control my mind—to find a strength that wouldn't come from physical practice but my mental practice. —S. Teague

Gratitude | THE FUTURE

Future insight...the future is shaping "now" possibility and imagination. Now creates the future now. The future is the cycle of birthing our better selves again and again.

All of my hope is in the "now" of the future. We are creating it and have the potential to change and overcome the stories we don't need to materialize or believe in anymore—stories of brutality, annihilation, and such to fill our religions and histories, and many of these propel us forward with fear for the future of humanity and the earth, and that means many people are fearful about now. They live in constant anxiety that the "now" we live in and the future will be devastating in some way. This type of worry and belief steals life away.

I am living for the future "now" that corrects the past mistakes and false dogma traditions that weren't ours to begin with. I believe in the potential for a future "now" of people who put aside differences to work together in respect and wonder for the preservation and continual change of the planet, for this sacred life.—Shana Thornton

Forgiveness

The phrase "Et tu, Brute?" from Shakespeare's "Julius Caesar" has always stuck in the back of my mind. Cliffs Notes made certain to make a predominant point about this phrase in the study of the play. Translating into "You too, Brutus?" or "And you, Brutus?" the measure of pain in the three simple words echoes in the minds of all those who have read it or seen the play.

We have all had a "Brutus!" or "Even you?" moment in our lives. The sharp pain of trust broken. The feeling of vulnerability, of exposure, of intimacy disregarded. The bond of a relationship broken or forever stained with hurt. Feeling helpless fucking sucks. The way out? The choice is yours.

Forgiveness should be given, BUT allow a renewal of trust to be at your discretion. Don't spend another minute at the hands of "Brutus" and release yourself from that pain. Forgive and be free. —S. Teague

Gratitude | BETRAYAL

It's easy for many people to be grateful for the high points and joys of life, and quite simply to train the psyche to reflect only joy, but the other parts of life will get through and push to the surface. Embracing both the highs and lows of life is more of a challenge. I cannot skip over the pain of betrayal and losses...we all suffer from it. My gratitude for betrayal is found in the lessons of discernment that the betrayals taught me.

People who thrive on betrayal and manipulation are dangerous to many of us who are working toward a helpful and creative purpose in life. We've all met people who simply didn't like us, but those generally aren't the people from whom we experienced betrayal. People who make us feel betrayed are usually friends or close family members, authority figures—they are people we trust, or we wouldn't feel betrayed. When a conflict arises, most of the time we don't get to remove ourselves completely from interacting with the people who are the source of the conflict or the person who did the betraying. Often, we must carefully choose when to be silent and when to interact with people who challenge and betray us. If we're lucky, this type of discernment leads to greater self-protection and finding true friends. —Shana Thornton

Questions to Ask Yourself | P A I N   I N F L U E N C E

Do you use the pain you feel from life's conflicts to create something helpful for yourself or others?

How does betrayal inspire or motivate you?

Do you become more compassionate about other perspectives based on what's happening in your life?

Are you less tolerant if your life isn't going the way you think it should be?

Does your creativity fizzle under certain circumstances?

We all meet people who could have been great teachers in our lives but instead chose to focus on their own mastery and how superior they feel. We have all shared life with people who want to hold us back.

How do you overcome these peoples' ideas for you if you must see these people daily?

When someone acts self-righteous toward you, does that motivate you in a creative way or a destructive way?

Is destruction a creative act for you? How? Are you able to control it?

How can you use the "negatives" in your life and make something funny, inspiring, creative, and/or profound out of them? —Shana Thornton

Gratitude | H E A L T H

My thankfulness about my health must include an awareness of the inevitability of death. Health is fragile. On the one hand, we control our health by how we treat our bodies and minds—what we eat, how we exercise, when we sleep, if we ingest other stuff (from supplements to ideas), and the access we have to healthy substances and ideas. On the other hand, any force of nature could suddenly and unexpectedly disrupt our health. This balance of luck and wise choices makes up our individual stories of health. In my life, I've been incredibly lucky and, after that, smart by paying attention to the needs of my body and mind. My intuition has guided me through minor injuries and avoided major problems. We wish for long, healthy lives, and many of us commit a large portion of living to ensuring that happens, barring any sudden accidents. The practices of running, yoga, and meditation have made me even more aware of not only my body's potential, but also how much my mind determines whether my experiences are healthy. — Shana Thornton

Be the Change | ANIMAL RESCUE

Our kittens, XRay, Honey, and Spike, became part of our family after a rigorous adoption process. I often joke that it's possibly easier to adopt children than our three cats, but I wanted them to stay together. They are litter mates, two brothers and a sister. In the winter, they enjoy climbing my Christmas trees and stalking the remote control helicopters that frequently fly around my house. They love to sleep all day and "make biscuits" with their paws on the pillow I am sleeping on at night. Their Christmas lists to Santa included tuna and catnip. Next on our adoption list is a puppy. The cats are thrilled. —S. Teague

Black & White

Black and white.
So much of my life I see in monochrome.
I can envision everything in grey scale.
Why?
Why would I choose a world without color?
In color, I find a covering of the true art.
Black and white allows me to see
The detail of the lines that make up the subject.
I can see it from the inside out.
I can see what is hidden under the makeup of color.
Every detail.
E.v.e.r.y. d.e.t.a.i.l.
The painting is the brush strokes.
The sculptor is the chisel.
The art is the lines, not the color.
Just as the song is the notes, not the instrument.
To see the beauty, look into the millions of steps taken to create
The final product.
The art lies in the work.
The work I see is black and white. —S. Teague

Progress | SURPRISE

I am a huge advocate of "loving you" and for being pleased
in your "now."
Yet, it's inevitable that our "now" comes with change.
Whether we are progressing or regressing,
our "now" is ever changing.
I got comfortable,
I settled in my "now."
A false comfort.
I have had an unsettling in my inner self for months now.
Tonight, I was able to define my unsettled feelings.
My "now" changed,
it moved right on without me.
While dissecting and discovering my "new now,"
my body said, "backbend."
I immediately said, "What did you say? Salt, you haven't changed that much."
I fought with myself. I didn't want to backbend.
I tried to talk myself into anything and everything but wheel pose during my yoga practice.
I caved in and trusted myself.
I set my timer on my phone, hoping to see
what my heart and mind were trying to show me.
I wasn't warm, I was panicked, and I wasn't breathing.
Yet, that first backbend was my best wheel pose to date.
I've grown, unknowingly, because I was "happy."
Do we do this often?
Do we not look for positive growth unless we have been through a

rough patch?

    My body and mind have been telling me for months
to see the growth,
that I was stuck.
I ignored it.
Even in a great place, I was unsettled and had no clue.
Tonight, I am welcoming my new "now,"
welcoming a new year.
I am learning to trust myself.
    To listen not only in the hard times but when life is good. —S. Teague

Gratitude | FAITH

One's faith is a private source of courage. Faith is discovered in the challenge, the facing of crisis, the darkness enveloping us and leaving us lost, and the free fall into unknown realms. Living is an act of faith—each day I go forward and try to become a better person by living a truer life to myself and the others around me. For me, faith in kindness, love, compassion, magic, luck, and more, was not found in recitations or other people's experiences, but it is represented in nature, where spring returns after winter and flowers bloom. To find my personal faith, I would need to come to terms with my inner wilderness, find my own guiding voice in the darkness, and make my way through personal rites of passage. To many Native American tribes, the turtle carries the world on her back. To me, the turtle metaphorically represents that the possibility of heaven exists here on earth, represented by the self carrying the home of the soul inside one's self. The turtle symbolizes the ultimate faith—life taking care of itself and meeting love along the way. Emerging from the cave or womb of life, we begin the slow patience of becoming and living (even when we think we're going quite fast, our life is but a tiny moment in the overall scheme of earth history), and we seek, like the turtle, the merger of land and water (spirit and matter; understanding and being unaware; thoughts and meditations). We need both to live. —Shana Thornton

Salty's 10 Laws

Always be kind.
Always see both sides.
Always forgive.
Always be careful with your trust.
Always be proud of who you are.
Always remember you are loved.
Always give love.
Always write.
Always make time for reading and art.
Always be Salty. —S. Teague

Empathy, Hand in Hand

I'm not any part of the wound, but I feel its anguish.
I'm not any part of the battle, but I see its annihilation.
I'm not any part of the disease, but I cry for its suffering.
I'm not any part of the discrimination, but I hear its fear.
I'm not any part of the demon, but I defy its anxiety.
I'm not any part of slavery, but I rally for its children.
I'm not any other but the part that holds you with an open heart.
I'm the one that weeps violently with you; though I wasn't with you then, I was inside you.
My heart leapt outside of me and into you and came back again, bleeding anew. —Shana Thornton

Gratitude | A JOURNEY

In "The Road Not Taken", Robert Frost wrote those lines that many people love to quote, about two roads diverging in a yellow wood. He expresses the conflict of the journey. We are choosing it, but it's actually life that's doing more choosing for us than we like to admit. We must leave behind paths that may have been beneficial or gratifying or fun. We cannot choose every path, but each path offers its own gifts of the seasons. Stay focused on what you can create on your path.

Winter sun wants spring and gives us a day for it. Rain drops cling to the grasses. Tree trunks allow us to slide along wet, mossy bark. The coyotes yip & howl in the distance. Deer hooves sink into mud. This winter sun beckons us out to the forests & trails to leave our marks. — Shana Thornton

Cave of Ancestors

The blessings of life often roll out in whispers,
Whispers to follow
A path, a trail, a window, a dance in a dream.
Find yourself on paths where your ancestors lived,
places you've never visited
though in your environment all along...
Places that seem as if they don't belong,
as if they've dropped in from another time,
to materialize,
preserved from centuries ago,
tucked in and hidden while everything changed
around it...while its metamorphosis
moved with slow resolve to hold onto
its ancient beauty. —Shana Thornton

SEASONS OF BALANCE

ABOUT THE AUTHORS

From the author, S. Teague:

"As a recovering approval addict, I turned to what seemed to be my place in this world and allowed myself to become self-aware by beginning a personal yoga journey in 2014. My inner artist and creator emerged. Through photography and prose, I came home to who I was always meant to be—an artist. As I took on many shapes and forms artistically, my approval obsession silenced while my art grew. I began to breathe in this new life for myself. All I needed was a little salt."

About Shana Thornton:

Shana Thornton is the owner of Thorncraft Publishing, an independent publisher of literature. She is the author of two novels, *Poke Sallet Queen & the Family Medicine Wheel* (2015) and *Multiple Exposure* (2012). Shana earned an M.A. in English from Austin Peay State University. She was the Editor-in-Chief of Her Circle Ezine, an online women's magazine. Shana teaches literature classes at Bethel University, and lives in Tennessee with her family. thorncraftpublishing.com

SEASONS OF BALANCE

www.ingramcontent.com/pod-product-compliance
Lightning Source LLC
Chambersburg PA
CBHW050123020526
44112CB00035B/2371